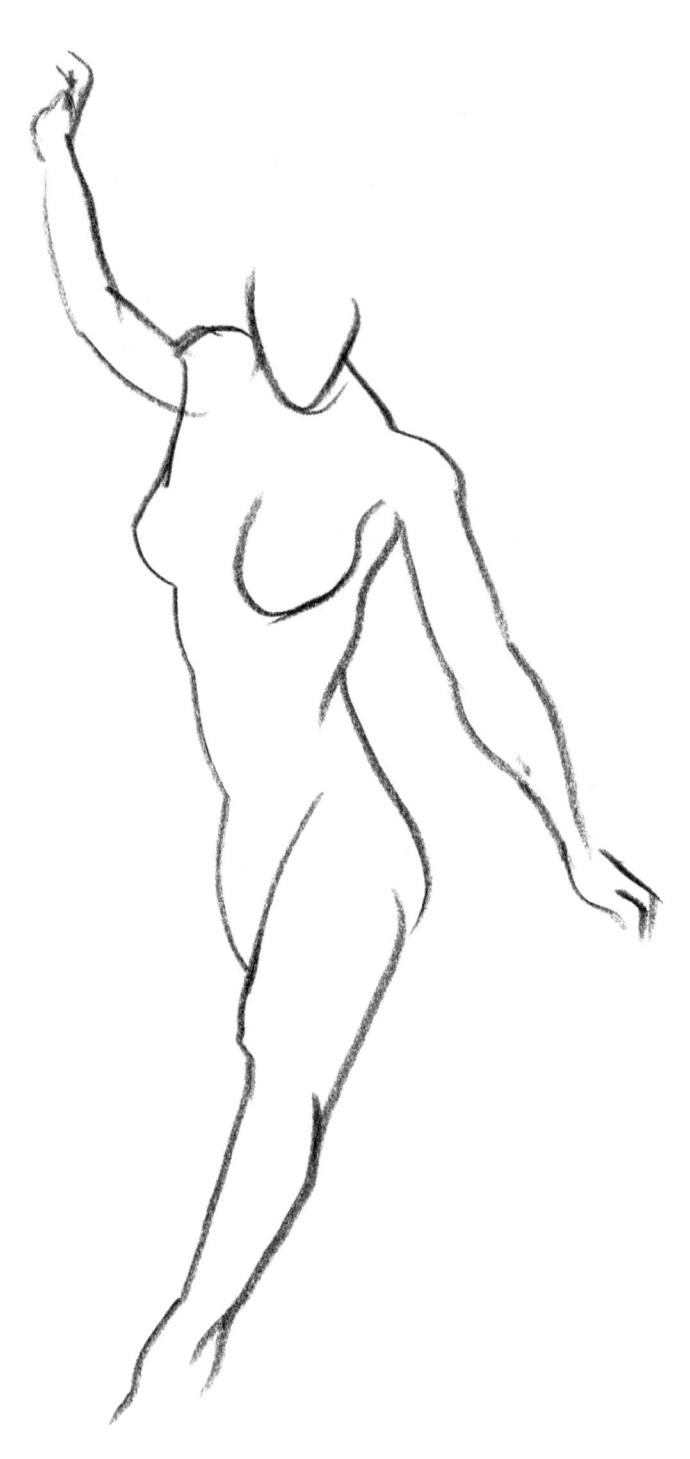

DRAWING THE HUMAN BODY

The Art of Figure Construction

ALON BEMENT

Featuring the Artwork of

Boyd Thomas

DRAWING THE HUMAN BODY: THE ART OF FIGURE CONSTRUCTION

Edited by James Bishop

Promethean Press
1846 Rosemeade Pkwy #192
Carrollton, TX 75007
www.promethean-press.com

Manufactured in the United States of America

ISBN 978-0-9810202-6-6

CREDITS: Sketches on pages 4, 8, 30, 36, 46, 53, the title page, and the cover are by Boyd Thomas; used with permission. Sketches on pages 2 and 22 by James Bishop; used with permission. Sketch on page 14 by Dave Kleinschmidt; used under Creative Commons license. Foreword image courtesy of the Vancouver Film School; used under Creative Commons License. Image on page 35 by Karl Weatherly courtesy of StockThink Photos. Image on page 13 courtesy of Stockbyte. Images on pages 33 and 98 courtesy of Goodshoot Photos. Image on pages 34 and 94 courtesy of Digital Vision. Image on page 45 courtesy of Getty Images. Images on pages 88 and 96 courtesy of Jupiter Images. Images on pages 90 and 91 courtesy of Pixland.

TABLE OF CONTENTS

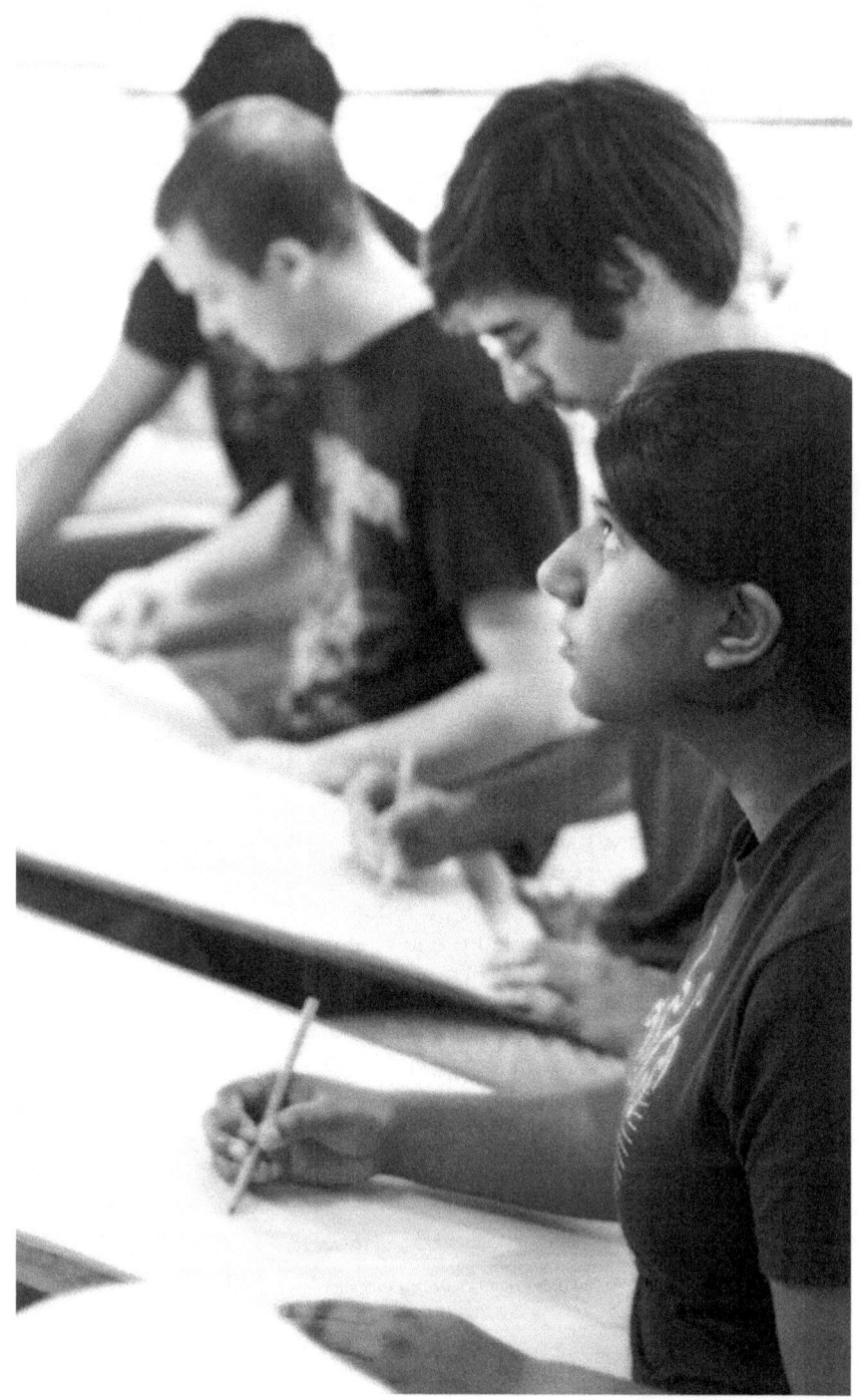

FOREWORD

What is life drawing? The average artist will answer this question by saying that it is a "tool of the trade." If he is bound by academic tradition he will admit that it is of *first* importance in art training. Many art teachers will agree with the academic artist. Others will hold that life drawing has a special, not a general, place in the scheme of art education and is, of course, necessary in certain fields, such as illustration, figure painting, portraiture, and costuming.

Valuable service is rendered to the world by him who recognizes a need, enters upon a course of experiments to meet it, and makes public the result of his experiments. This is what Professor Bement has done, as set forth in the following pages. He has given one answer to the question at the head of this article, and has made a contribution that will be of direct and practical value to art education. It is the result of a need at Columbia University of finding some method of teaching life drawing whereby the students in costume design could gain a sufficient knowledge of the human figure to meet the requirements of their craft. Many of the students were inexperienced in drawing and none of them could give the time to a professional art school drill. The regular traditional method that leaned upon anatomy, with accuracy as an aid, failed with this class of students. It was necessary to find another way. This book shows us the way.

Accuracy in itself is not art, and to attempt to make it the aim by freehand methods is a waste of effort, except possibly for those intending to be professional artists. To most young students accuracy is practically unattainable and, even if it could be attained, its value would be doubtful, for in figure drawing the important things to appreciate are *life* and *action*.

Action is expressed by the *direction* of the lines, and life lies in the *quality* of the drawn line. Life is felt; it never comes through imitation. In Japanese sketch books of the last century are line drawings of figures and animals where life and action are given by one or two lines. Children draw readily and naturally in this way—by seeing the subject as a whole. After that is realized it is easy to add details.

Freehand drawing would progress farther if we looked upon it as *expression* rather than *imitation*. Students will draw better, if they are led to appreciate fine rhythm, good spacing, and unity in masterpieces of line,

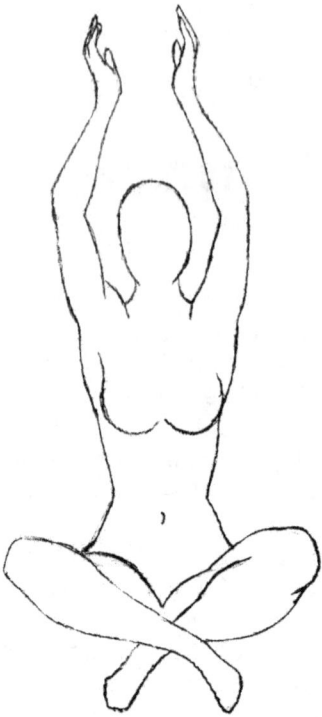

not only in drawings, but in architecture, sculpture, and pattern, and if they are encouraged to create these qualities by simple exercises with brush and pencil.

Professor Bement has taken advantage of natural aptitudes and has called into action those creative powers that will work if we will only give them a chance. He is not proposing any short cuts, but shows that there is more than one road to excellence. His book will bring a sense of freedom and courage to many young students and should be most appreciatively received by the teachers of art.

ARTHUR WESLEY DOW
Professor of Fine Arts
Columbia University

PREFACE

The methods of drawing presented in this book are based on four assumptions:

1. That it is easier to draw the figure in action than in the half action employed in life classes, or in the rigid bi-symmetrical attitudes shown in books of drawings and anatomy.
2. That, except when seen from the front, the action of the body may be expressed in nearly every instance by two lines—a convex and a concave curve.
3. That the beginner should be instructed in drawing the figure as a whole before he studies the detached parts, because drawing the detached parts first has a tendency to establish in the mind these parts in a position that is difficult to combine with the other parts of the figure when in action.
4. That the time employed in making each stroke in a drawing should be *limited*, for great artists have been masters of technique, and technique presupposes skill, and skill, in turn, presupposes speed.

We have, therefore, in the following chapters, laid great stress on the reduction of the time allowed for each stroke from the beginning. We have reversed the usual procedure, believing that the inherent good qualities of the first rapidly-drawn line will be retained through the entire procedure. We believe also that it is better to make five drawings rapidly in order to procure one good one, than to spend the same time making corrections on the first.

While this book is designed primarily to meet the needs of students of high schools and colleges who cannot reach life classes, it is confidently believed that it will be of equal assistance to students working from the live model, as it is a record of the exact procedure of a very successful life class at Columbia University.

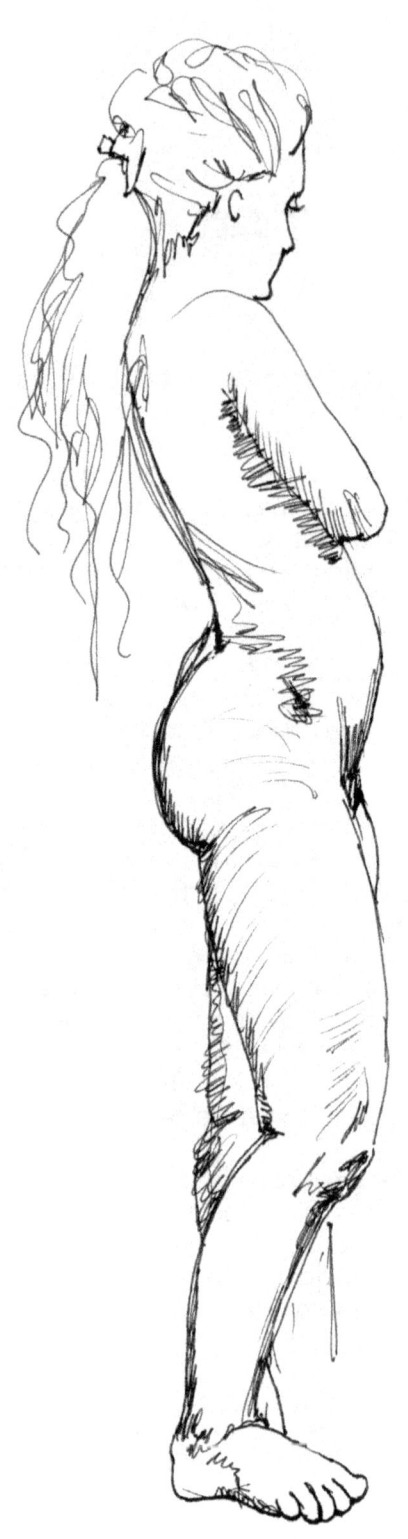

CHAPTER ONE
THE FIGURE IN PROFILE

To draw the action of the body from the side only two construction lines are necessary, one for the front of the body, and the other for the back. According to the directions given below, make the construction lines very carefully but quite pale. The actual lines of the figure should be made with single strokes for each of the concave and convex curves. A new beginning should be made for each curve. The strokes should be made in the speediest possible manner, without going over any of the lines a second time, or making corrections of any kind. Pause only long enough between strokes to decide the length and direction of the next stroke.

DIRECTIONS

Draw two curved lines AB and CD five inches long, having the point A directly over B, C three-quarters of an inch from A, and D one-quarter of an inch from B.

The line AB may be said to represent the front of the figure. It is composed of *one concave* and *three convex* lines.

Beginning at the top of AB, draw a rather long *convex* line representing the chest; just below it a short line representing the abdomen, and a long one representing the front of the thigh, and the only *concave* line on the front of the figure from the knee to the foot.

Line CD may be said to represent the back of the figure. It is made up of *four convex* lines, *one double curve*, and *one concave line*.

Beginning at the top, draw a fairly long *convex line* representing the figure's back. Extend it well in from the construction line at the waist, then draw a very short *concave line* (in the middle of the back), and another short but very full *convex line* representing the thigh. Below this draw a *double curve* from the thigh to the back of the knees, followed by a *convex curve* to the ankle.

Repeat the exercise twelve times, allowing five minutes for a drawing. Use a different pencil for each drawing.

Relative measurements will be given in proper time, the idea being, at first, to keep the student's mind entirely on the action of the figure and the simplest contours.

QUESTIONS: Describe the construction lines to be used in drawing in the true profile of the body. How many simple curves in the front contour? How many in the back contour? Where is the first concave curve found? Where is the double curve located? Why are no relative measurements given?

NOTE ONE

In giving a lesson to a class without a model, the teacher should read the directions aloud (or give some explanation in her own words) and then make a drawing on the board illustrating the exact procedure of the lesson. It is helpful to count for the convex or concave strokes. For instance, one, for the convex line of the chest, pause; two, for the convex line of the abdomen, pause, and so on. The counting and the pauses show the time allowed between the strokes, and make clear in the mind of the student the idea of separating each stroke from the one following.

With the model, the same procedure is helpful, but not absolutely necessary. Care should be taken, during the early lessons, to pose the model at the end of the studio, in such a manner as to assure as nearly as possible the same pose to the whole class. After Chapter 10, with the student having already drawn the figure in several positions, the model can be posed in the center of the room and the students placed in a circle about her.

NOTE TWO

If the students are studying the figure only as costume designers, a more definite scale of measurements than those included in Chapter One should be given. The following proportions are in use in several studios, and have been found to be of practical value: Draw a vertical line eight inches long, divide the right side of the upper half into fourths, the left side of the upper half into thirds, and the lower half into two parts; draw the construction lines described in Chapter One, between the point marked for the shoulders and the lower end of the vertical line, as exemplified in the accompanying diagram. The head will then fill the one-inch space at the upper end, and the other divisions of the figure will fall approximately on the points designated.

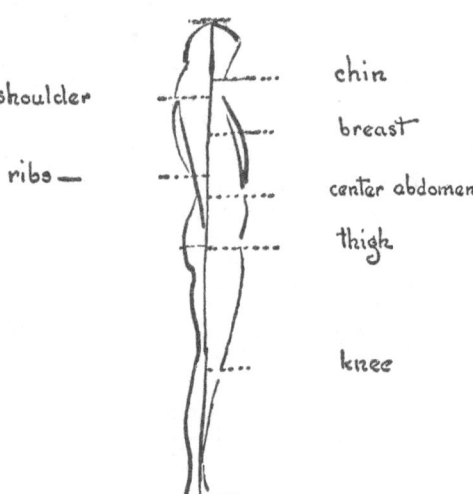

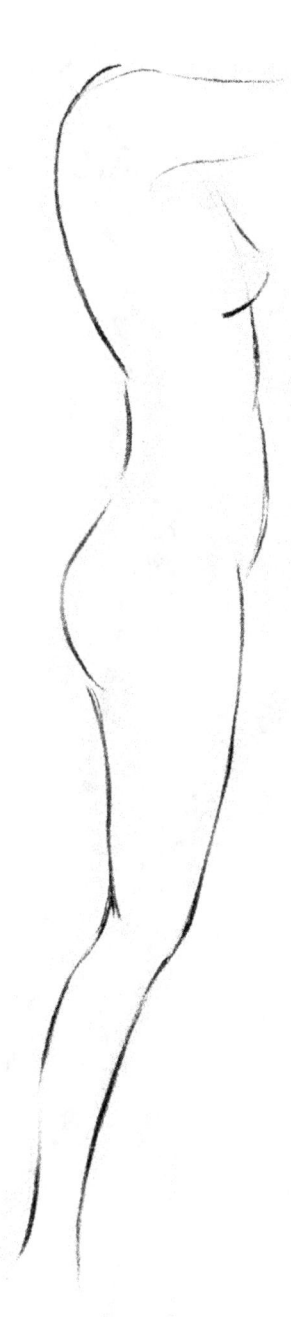

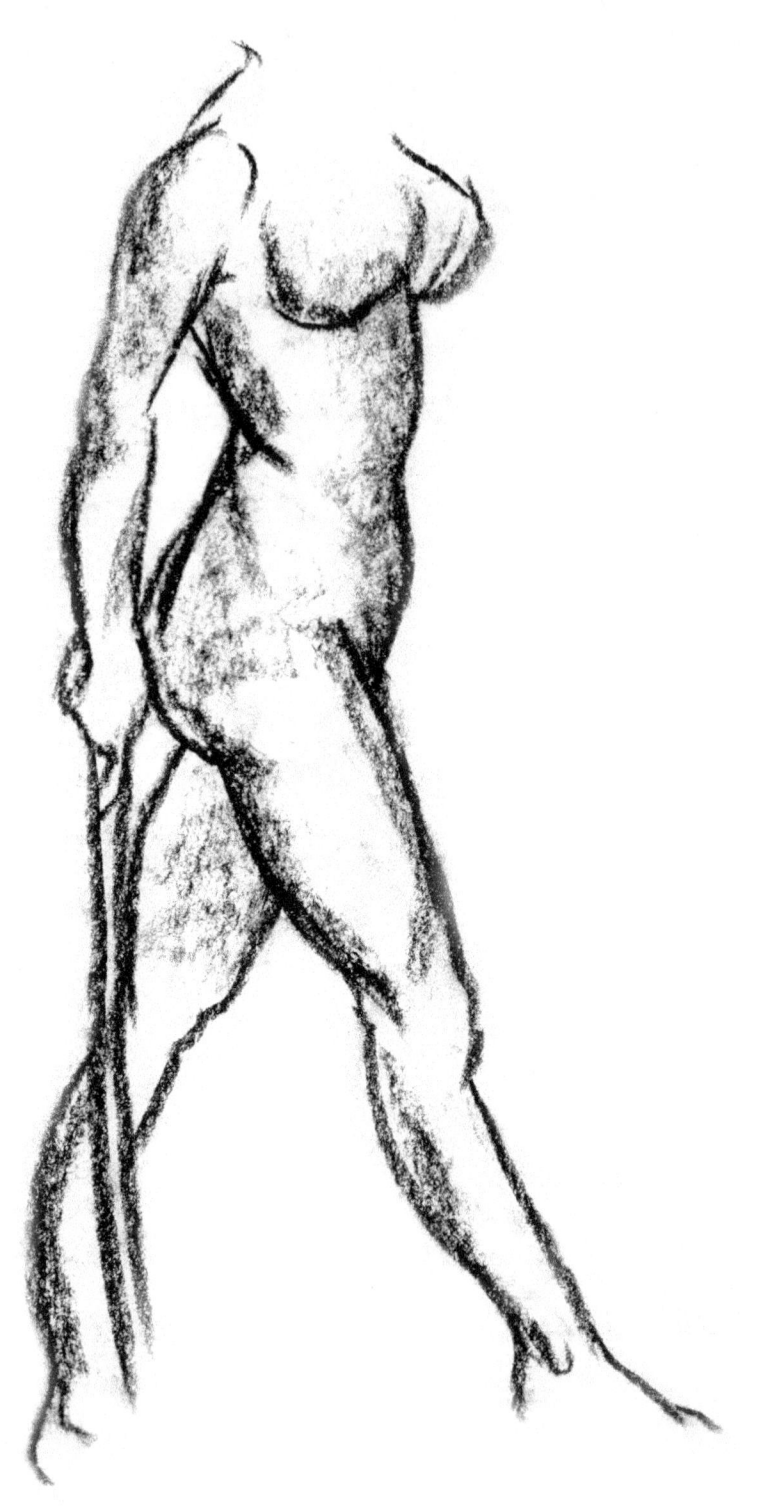

CHAPTER TWO
THE ARM IN PROFILE

It is interesting to note that the construction lines for the arm are almost exactly the same as those of the body, except that they are shorter and are turned to a horizontal position.

Draw the construction lines slowly and with care, the actual lines of the arm with speed and power, one stroke for each curve, with no corrections of any kind. The arm drawn thus will attach to the figure in several positions—extended forward, lifted up, or hanging down.

DIRECTIONS

Draw construction lines AB and CD two and one-quarter inches long; C being one-half inch from A, and D one-quarter of an inch from B.

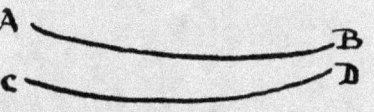

Line AB may be said to represent the upper side of the arm. It is made up of one double and two convex curves. Beginning at A, draw a short but full convex line representing the deltoid muscle of the shoulder. Then draw a slightly longer and very flat convex line for the top of the biceps, and below that the double curve of the forearm to the wrist.

Line CD may be said to represent the under side of an extended arm and, except for a slight bulge at the elbow and the forearm below, it will serve just as it is.

Make ten or twelve drawings combining Chapters One and Two, with the arms in different positions. Complete each in five minutes. Do not erase or redraw any part. Use a soft pencil with a blunt point.

QUESTIONS: How do the construction lines of Chapters One and Two differ? Where is the double curve in this case? Where is the concave line located? Which position of the arm do you like the best of those that you have drawn? Which is the easiest to draw?

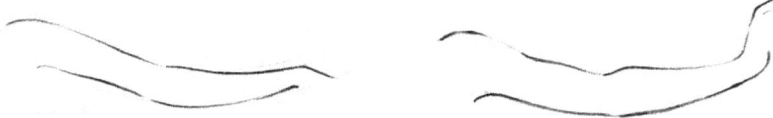

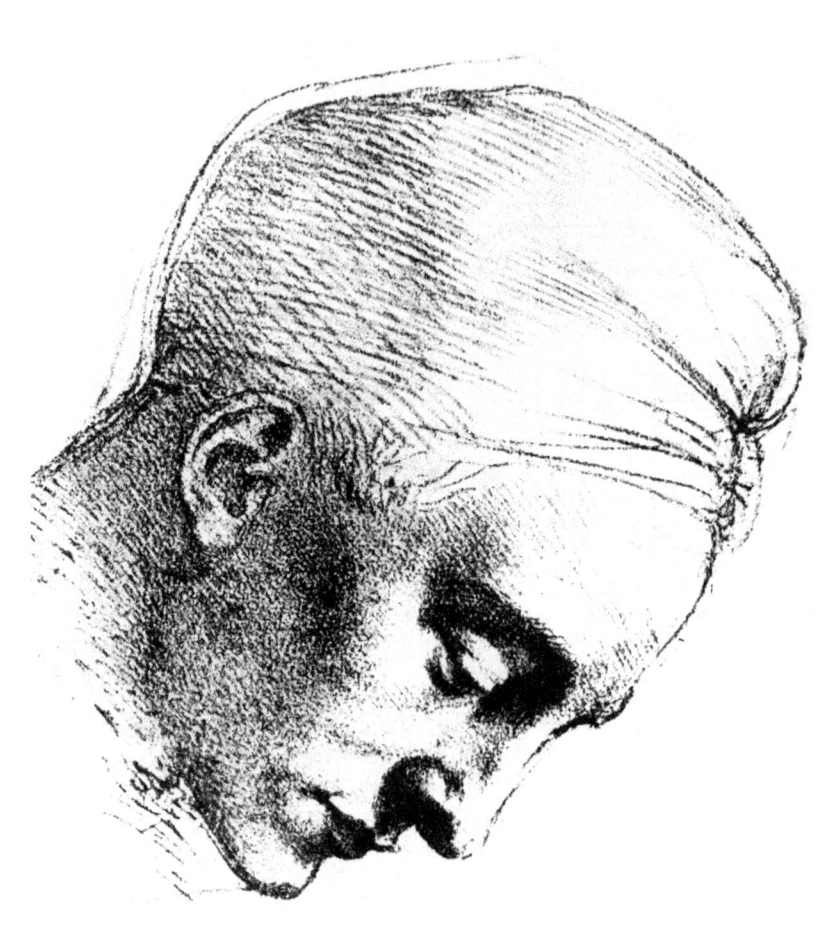

CHAPTER THREE
THE HEAD IN PROFILE

In drawing the head in profile disregard, for the time being, the eyes and the mouth. Think of the head only as a comparatively round decorative form, with one side flat, but with the sort of roundness that seems to be based on a square rather than on a circle.

DIRECTIONS

Draw a square with the sides three-quarters of an inch long.

Beginning at B draw a convex line a little outside A to a point somewhat above C. This line may represent the top and back of the head (including the hair), while the line BD represents the profile of the face with the point of the chin at D. The first third of the line DC represents the line under the chin (No. 1).

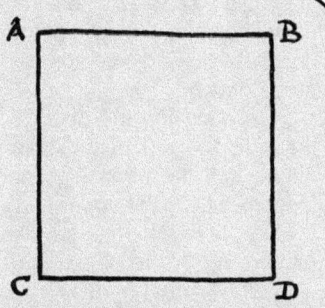

Repeat this exercise, but tip the square forward until it is at an angle of forty-five degrees from the perpendicular. Attached to the figure in Chapter One, it will be found that the front of the neck almost entirely disappears, while the line at the back is extended until it becomes a part of the convex curve of the back (No. 2).

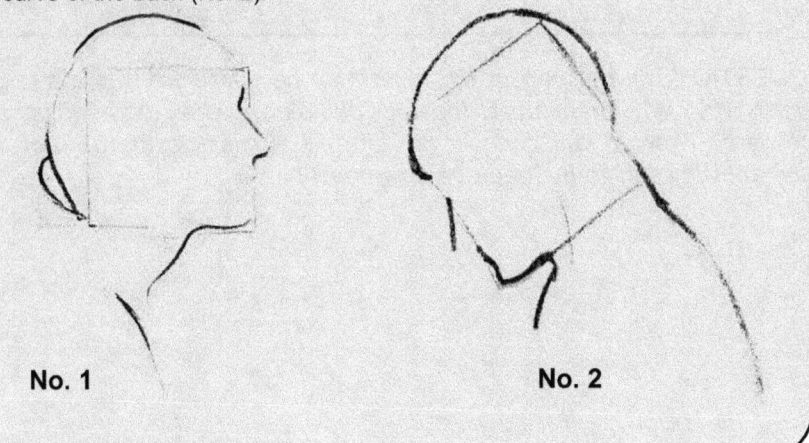

No. 1   No. 2

Repeat this exercise by tipping the square back to an angle of forty-five degrees at the left of the perpendicular. In this position it is the back of the neck that almost entirely disappears, while the front is extended and becomes a convex curve that connects with the bent-in end of the chest (No. 3).

Draw each head at least five times. Alternate the direction in which they face. Do not attempt to draw the eyes or mouth, for in so doing the mind is taken off the whole outline, which is the most important thing to remember.

In drawing the head it is not necessary to draw the entire square each time. It should be carefully kept in mind that the face line should always be drawn in order to establish the *angle* at which the head is to be drawn.

In attaching the head that is thrown back to the top of the figure, it will be found that the throat line does not connect exactly to the upper end of the chest. It is necessary then to bend in slightly the upper end of the chest line to meet the line of the throat.

It must be remembered that the body should be drawn *first, the arms next,* and *the head last,* for, although the head may direct the action of the body, this action is expressed by the long lines of the trunk, and the head, arms and feet are but completions of the movement.

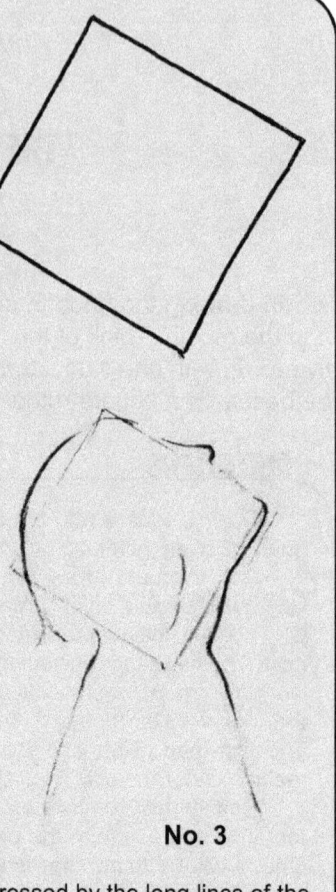

No. 3

QUESTIONS: What part of the head may be considered as a straight line? Why? What happens to the back of the neck when the head is bent forward? How do you connect the top of the chest to the front of the throat? Why should the head be drawn last?

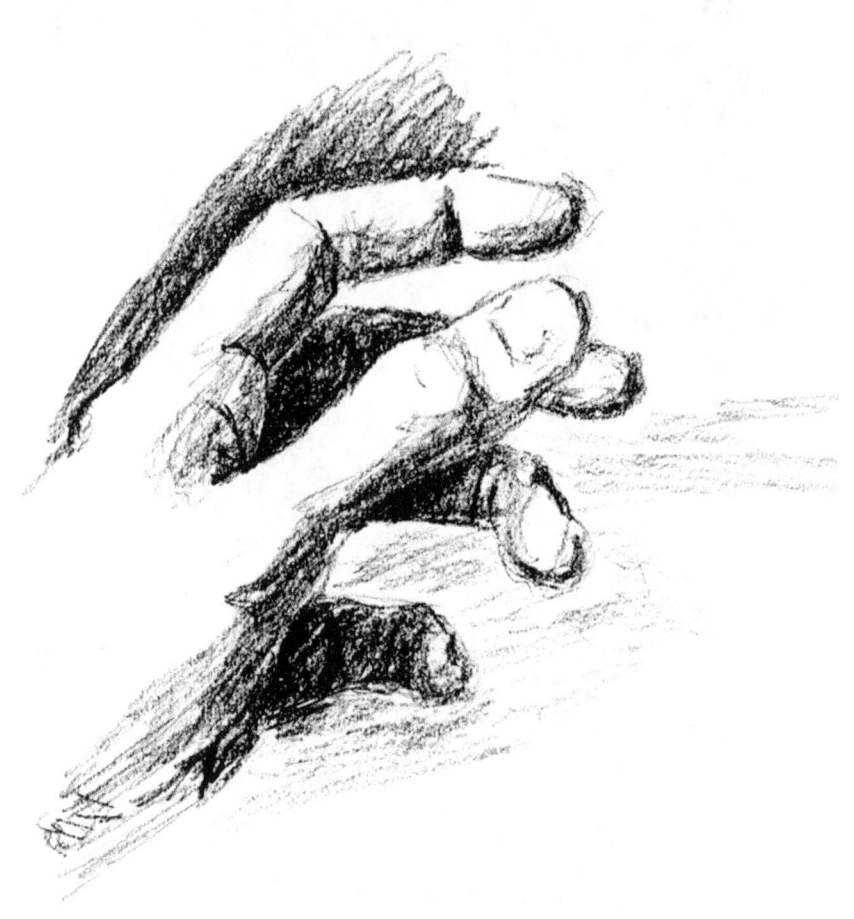

CHAPTER FOUR
THE HAND, THE FOREARM, AND SIMPLE MEASUREMENTS

Robert Fletcher, in compiling the man measurements for the Provost Marshal's Office at Washington, reported 115 published methods of man measurements. Some of them were in use before the Christian era. In a translation from the Greek, by Leonardo da Vinci, we find the following formula: "Nature, in the composition of the human form, has so ordained that the face, from the chin to the highest point where the hair begins, is one-tenth of the whole stature. These proportions obtain in the hand, measured from the wrist to the front of the middle finger. The head from the chin to the top of the scalp is an eighth; from the top of the chest to the highest point of the forehead is a sevent; from the nipples to the top of the scalp is one-fourth of the whole."

"If the length of the face be divided into three equal parts, the first intersection will determine the place of the nostrils, the second, the point where the eyebrows meet; the ear, likewise, a third of the length of the face."

A later, far less exact, but extremely serviceable and easily remembered scale of measurement, is one in which each extremity is estimated to be three-quarters of the part above. Thus the hand is three-quarters of the forearm, the forearm is three-quarters of the upper arm. The foot is three-fourths the length of the lower leg, and the lower leg three-quarters of the upper. The long thighbone is equal to the distance from the thigh to the shoulder, and the normal hand and arm reach to a point half way down the thigh. These measurements are not exact, but they come near enough to make a very practical working basis until time can be taken to study the more complex systems.

The Greek ideal of eight heads to the figure seems too high for the average figure of today. It is advisable for the student to make the head more nearly the normal size, which is about one-seventh of the height of the whole body.

DIRECTIONS

The construction lines for the forearm are like those of the whole arm, the only difference being that they are farther apart.

In this lesson, however, the student will consider the hand as part of the forearm, as an extension of the graceful curves that make up its outline. Do not think of the hand as being made up of fingers, but think of the curves that make up its contour.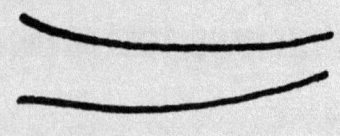

Draw your own hand and arm, held before you, in five or six different positions. Draw each time as though the line of the arm passed through the hand and came out along the fingers. (By the use of the mirror your own left hand may be made to seem like the right of another person.)

The foot, for the time being, may be considered as having one straight line along the bottom, and another up the back of the ankle. With a slight extension of the heel this line will be sufficient to establish the action of the foot until there is time to study it more carefully.

QUESTIONS: Describe the da Vinci theory of measurement. Describe a simpler system. What measurement is exactly the same length as that of the long thighbone? Compare the foot with the lower leg. According to the da Vinci theory, locate the center of your last drawing. Have you ever seen anyone who is eight heads high? What is the normal size of the head today?

Describe what the beginner's attitude toward the details of the hands should be. Should the lines of the hands be drawn with those of the forearm or separately? Describe how the lines on the opposite side of the forearm seem to connect with each other. Do you think that this is one of the reasons why the human figure is considered more beautiful than any other?

How long is the hand compared with the forearm? The forearm compared with the upper arm? How far down the thigh does the arm and hand extend? What is the longest bone in the body? What other measurement is exactly like it? How long is the foot compared with the lower leg? How many heads high is the average modern figure? How many heads high is the Greek ideal?

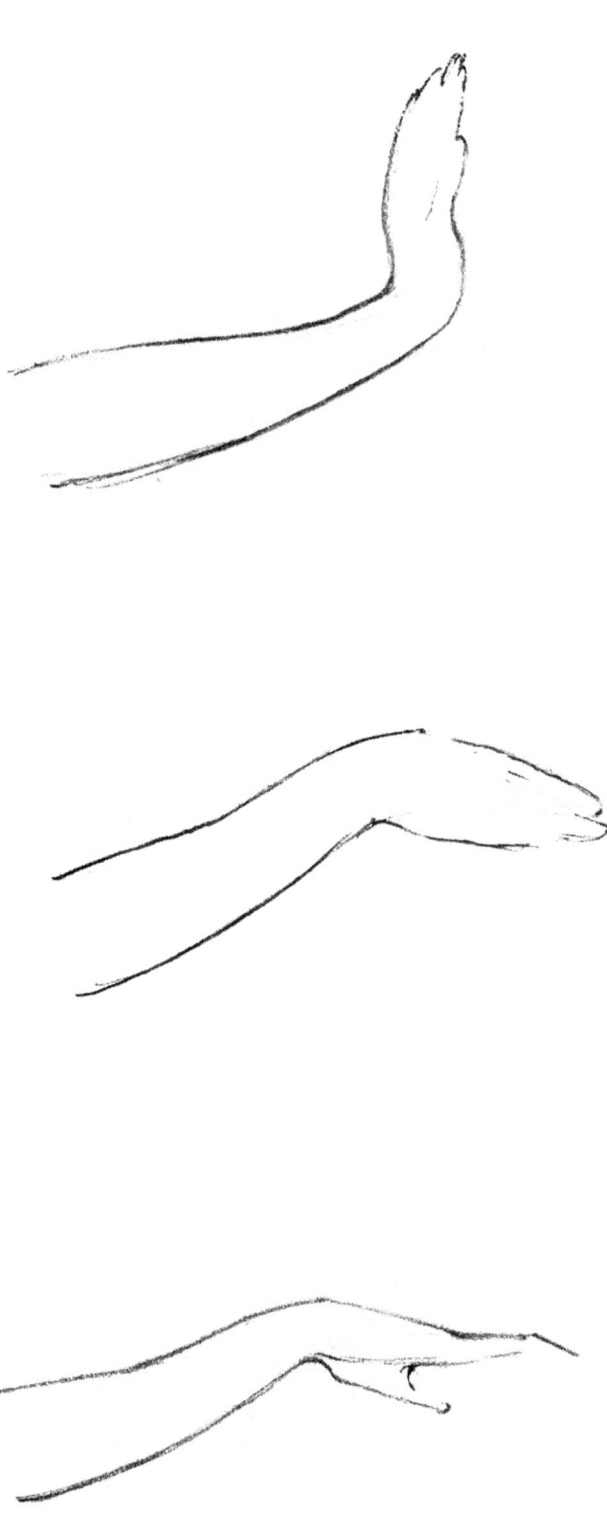

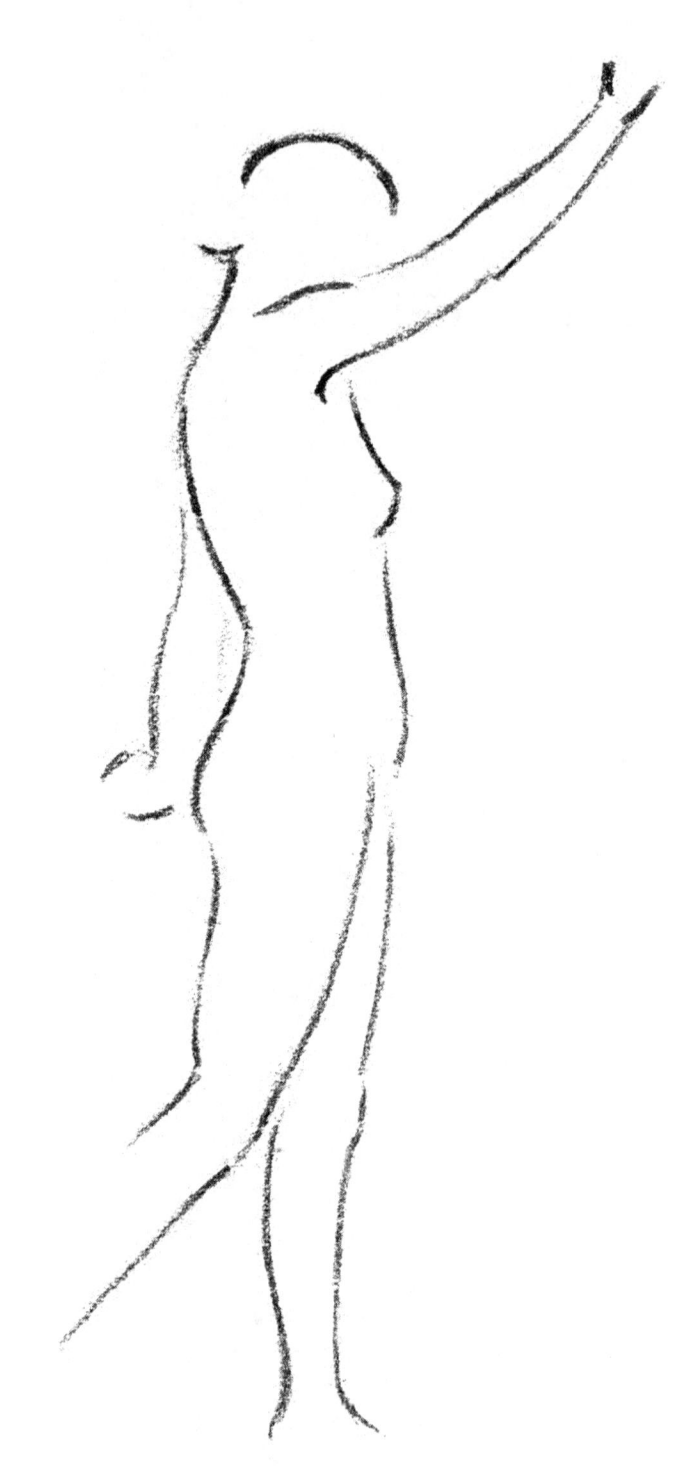

CHAPTER FIVE
VARIATIONS OF THE PROFILE

The construction lines for Chapter Five are simply a combination of those of Chapters One to Four. When the feet are separated, as they are in this case, the figure is constructed above the foot that bears the weight, as it is of first importance to establish the center of gravity, thus placing the action on its most immovable pedestal. The one that bears the least weight should be drawn last. It could be moved an inch or two in either direction without disturbing the balance of the rest of the figure. To move the first even a fraction of an inch would mean moving the whole.

Draw the trunk first, as in Chapter One, then the arms, the left leg, the head, and finally, the right leg. The left arm is the only new element in construction. It is shown bent slightly in reverse at the elbow, as often happens in the feminine figure. The construction line for it should be bent also, following its inside contour.

DIRECTIONS

Draw two curved lines AB and CD and complete the body as in Chapter One.

Draw the construction lines for the arms as in Chapter Two.

Draw the construction lines for the head as in Chapter Three.

Repeat this exercise ten times and reserve the two drawings that seem to you to be the best.

It is interesting to observe that the lines in this figure flow into each other in such a manner that they seem to be connected, and to give the figure the feeling of being very smooth and solid.

QUESTIONS: In what important particulars does this figure differ from that described in Chapters One to Four? Which foot should be drawn first and why? Does that affect the construction lines? How many heads high is this figure? Is the right arm exactly the right length? Is the distance from the knee to the thigh correct compared with the distance from the thigh to the shoulder? What are the new elements in this chapter?

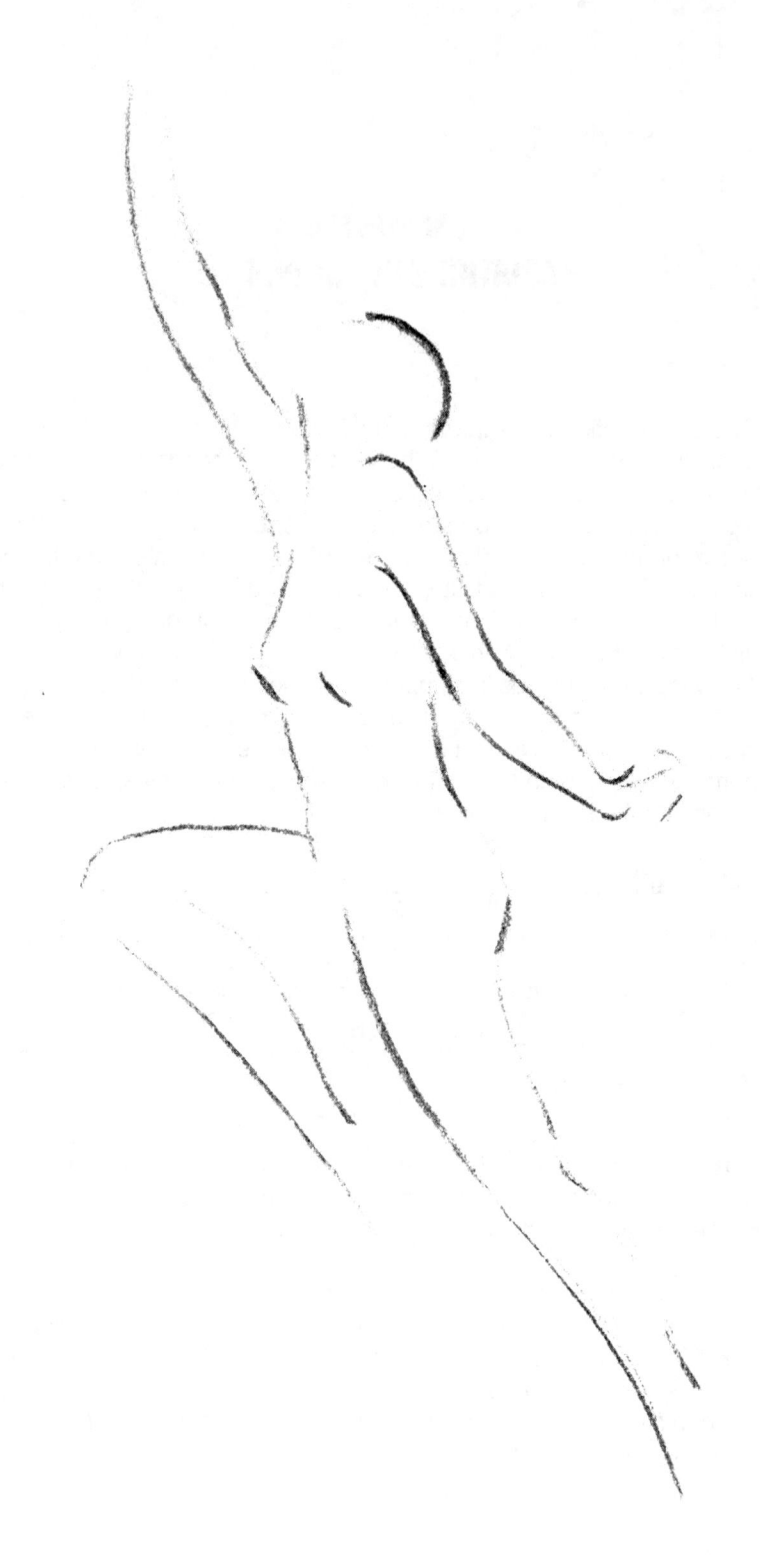

CHAPTER SIX
DYNAMIC FIGURE

The construction lines for Chapter Six are similar to those of Chapter One, except that they are more curved. Owing to the feet being partially raised from the ground and the action very extreme, there is no necessity of a careful balance of weight. It is conceivable that with the feet off the ground the body may have any relation to them desired. It is necessary, however, in order to give the appearance of speed, to have as many of the contours as possible slant in the same direction. The figure on the opposite page is an excellent example of this. The lines seem to lift the figure up toward the left. The figure was drawn without a model in considerably less than the required four minutes.

DIRECTIONS

Draw the construction lines as in Chapter One, only reverse, tip them forward, and make them more curved.

Draw the front of the body first and then the back, the arms, and the head. Draw the upraised leg last. It is made up of a convex and a concave curve at the front, and a double curve and convex line at the back, exactly as in Chapter One. Repeat ten times. In the first five trials reverse every other one. In the last five make the figure tip backward instead of forward, every other time.

Draw a dynamic figure of your own invention.

QUESTIONS: Explain how the lines, flowing from one to another, seem to add to the beauty and feeling of rhythm in the figure. Is drawing made somewhat easier by understanding these continuous lines? Explain how. Is the lower leg in the right proportion to the upper one? Is the head too large or too small for the other proportions?

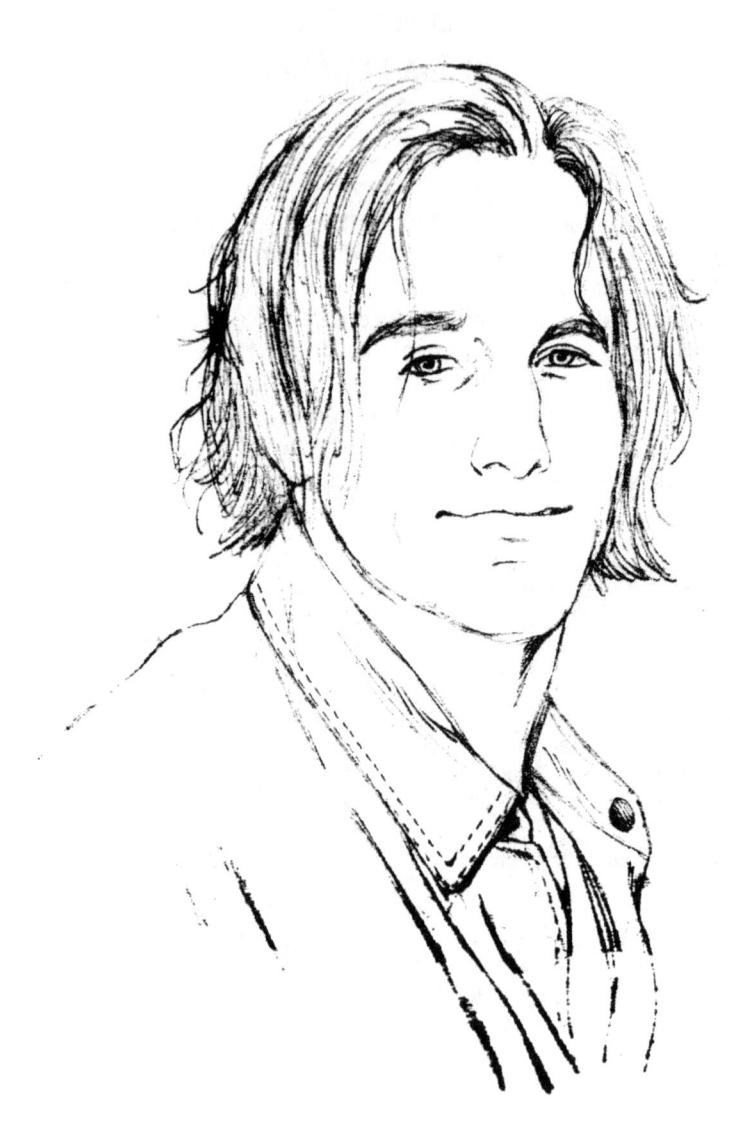

CHAPTER SEVEN
THE HEAD - FRONT VIEW

The head is represented as being circular in form when not seen in profile. There are positions in which it seems almost round although it is really much longer than it is wide. The bony structure from the front, on the same level as the observer, is elliptical or egg-shaped. As the head turns from this position it becomes wider through the center until it reaches the true profile, where it fits more nearly into a square. Up to the point where the cheekbone disappears behind the nose, the circular form seems to serve best. Beyond that point the square character is very apparent. In drawing the neck great care must be exercised, for the lines not only *attach* the head to the body, but they *support* it and give it its balance. Turn the head as you will, at least one of the two strong cords that stretch from below the ear to the center of the top of the breastbone will bulge out and supplement the outlines of the head. The two cords may be said to form a V that sets point down on the top of the breastbone. In this cup rests the head, and as it is raised or lowered or turned, the lines of the cords follow exactly the lines of the cheeks and extend their contours downward.

When the head and neck are seen directly from in front, the cords do not show as part of the outline, but when the body is turned or the head is bent to the side, one will always appear.

DIRECTIONS

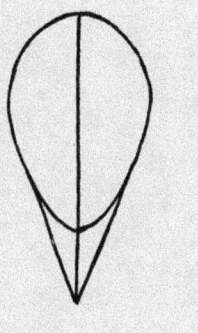

Draw lightly in a vertical position an egg-shaped form about an inch and a half high and one inch wide.

Extend the outlines of the sides downward until they meet in an angle. This drawing will serve as a basis for the drawing of the head, and will represent the form spoken of above.

(If the eyes are to be drawn, they will be placed on a horizontal line half way up this ellipse.)

Draw in the hair by drawing a circular line beginning at the top of neck cords and going well above the ellipse of the head. Beginning at the same point draw a second line inside the first line.

The face is represented by the space that is left.

Draw yourself in a mirror in three positions— or get another student to pose for you.

Try to draw eight heads, from poses, in thirty minutes.

Do not draw any of the features, for the idea is to keep the mind entirely on the shapes of the outline.

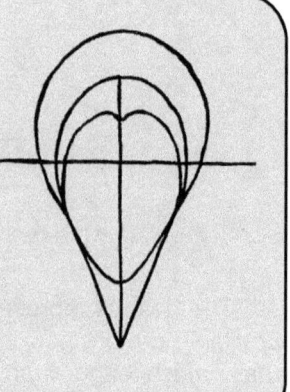

QUESTIONS: From in front what is the characteristic shape of the head? Describe the construction lines. Where in this egg-shaped form should the eyes be placed? How does drawing the hair affect the position of the eyes? When the head is tipped forward and turned a little to the side, what is the general form? When does the head most nearly resemble a square? How are the cords that connect the head to the breastbone important in drawing the head? When do they become part of the outline of the neck? Do you think that drawing them would assist the student to make the action of the head and neck convincing?

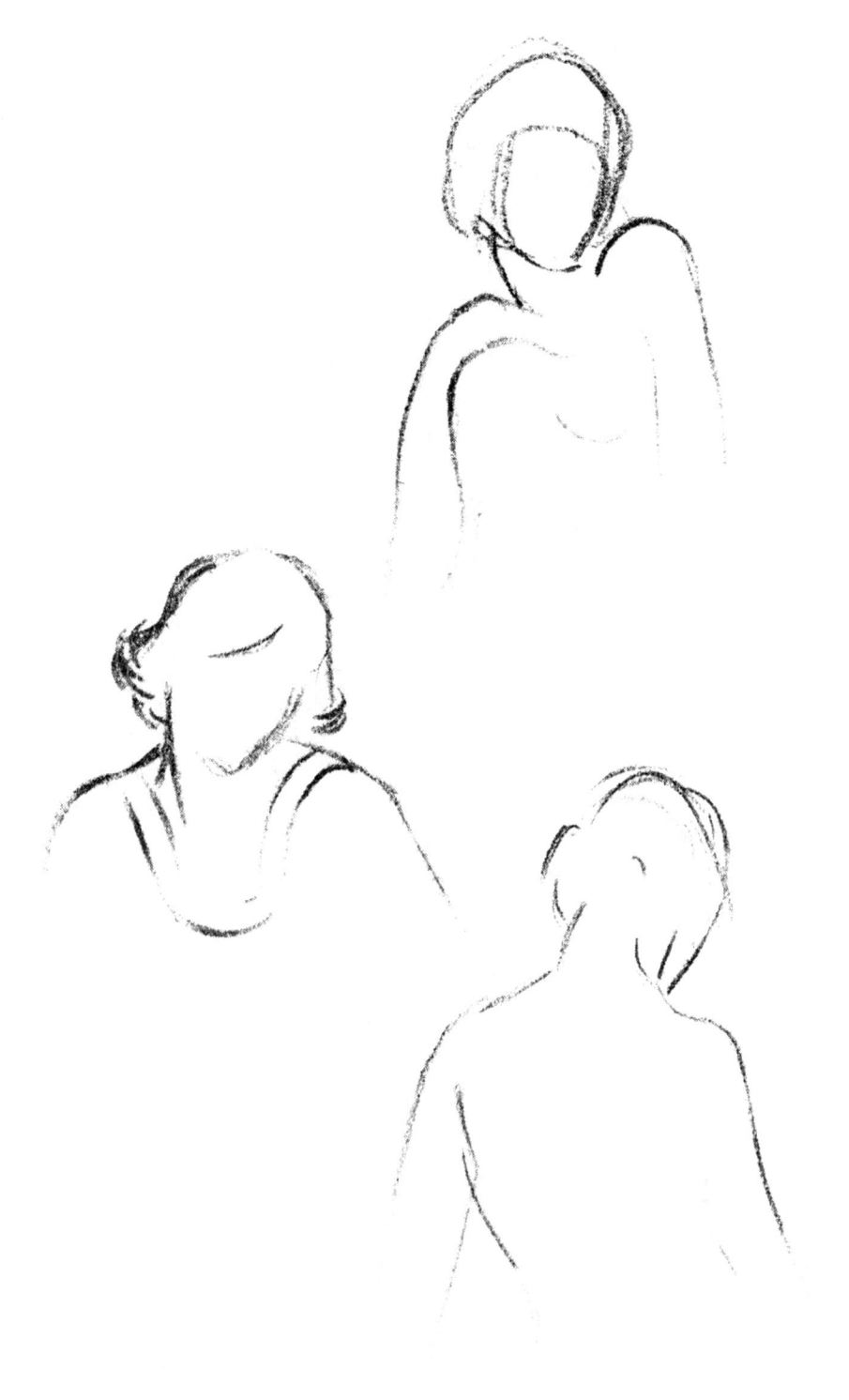

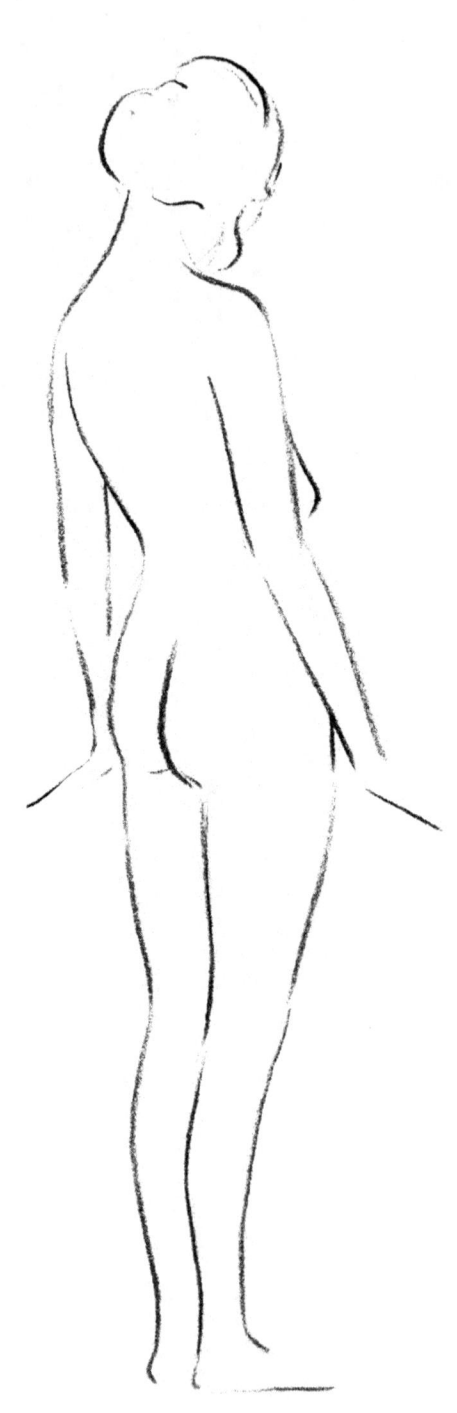

CHAPTER EIGHT
THE BACK - THREE-QUARTERS VIEW

The construction lines for Chapter Eight are the same as in Chapter One except that they are a little farther apart. The figure should be drawn as before—the body first— as if it had no arms or head; then the arms, and last, the head. It is interesting to observe how well the outspread position of the hands has been expressed by two straight lines.

Repeat the directions of Chapter One, but instead of using three-quarters of an inch, use one inch at the top and one-half of an inch at the bottom.

DIRECTIONS

Draw the head on an oval form somewhat higher than it is wide.

Draw the figure five times, changing the position of the arms each time.

Draw the figure four times, facing to the left.   Allow four minutes to each drawing.

Sharpen a soft pencil to a chisel point and draw on the same drawing, first with the narrow edge, and then with the wide edge. Hold the pencil well back from the point each time.

QUESTIONS: HOW does this figure differ in construction from Chapter One? Are the concave curves in the same place? If the head were thrown back, would the figure be bent more or less? Explain why. Would it be possible for a figure to show the shoulders as they are in this figure, and the hips in pure profile? In what ancient art were the figures represented in this position? Does drawing the figure in that pose present greater difficulties to the artist, or less? Do you think it was on account of prevailing art standards that the Egyptian artists drew the figure in a twisted pose, or was it because they could not draw the actual position of the figure?

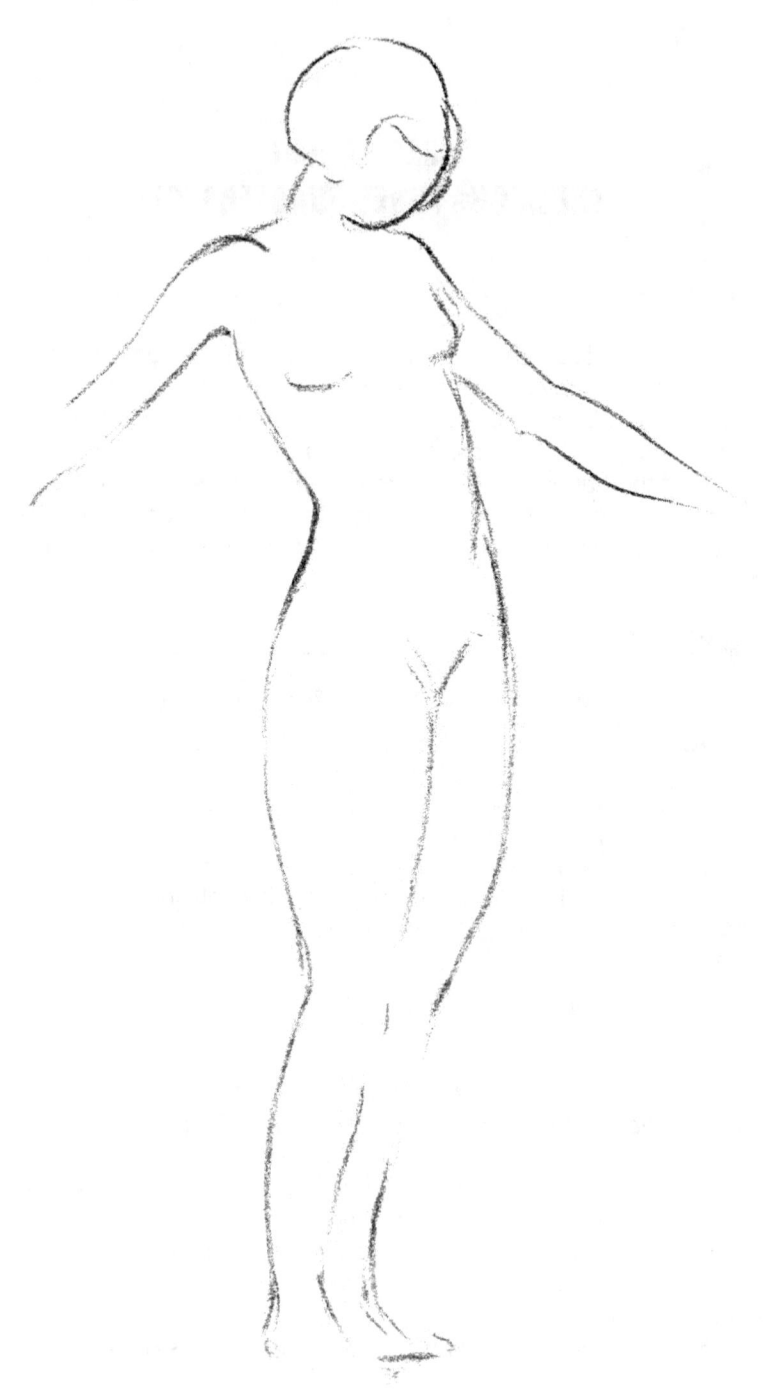

CHAPTER NINE
THE FRONT - THREE-QUARTERS VIEW

The construction lines for Chapter Nine are the same as those of Chapter One, except that they are a little farther apart. The head, in this case, can be expressed by something very like a circle, for it is turned enough to have the cheek, instead of the profile, count as part of the outline. It is interesting to note that the back of the neck is convex, which adds to the action of the figure, and if continued down it will join the line of the side at the waist.

The lines of the hips are very interesting, as they curve in, in such a manner that they point directly to the outside of the ankles on the opposite side. To a close observer it will become apparent that the long *convex* line on the front of the figure was extended up into the space occupied by the head until it almost touched the reverse curve that represents the action of the upper part of the back and neck.

DIRECTIONS

Repeat the directions given in Chapter One.

Draw the figure five times facing to the left, and five times facing to the right.

Draw from memory the first position. Draw the figure four times, with the arms and head in a different position each time.

Select the three best drawings and compare them with the drawings made in Chapter One.

Be sure to use four different pencils each day. Change the kind of paper on which you draw as often as possible.

QUESTIONS: Describe the construction line used for the head when the cheek appears as part of it. How does the convex line at the back of the neck help the action of the whole figure? With what line does it seem to connect? Why were the hips especially mentioned? Does the line on most hips seem to do the same thing but in a less degree? Is it more interesting to draw the figure in action or in repose? Why? Which is the easier? Why?

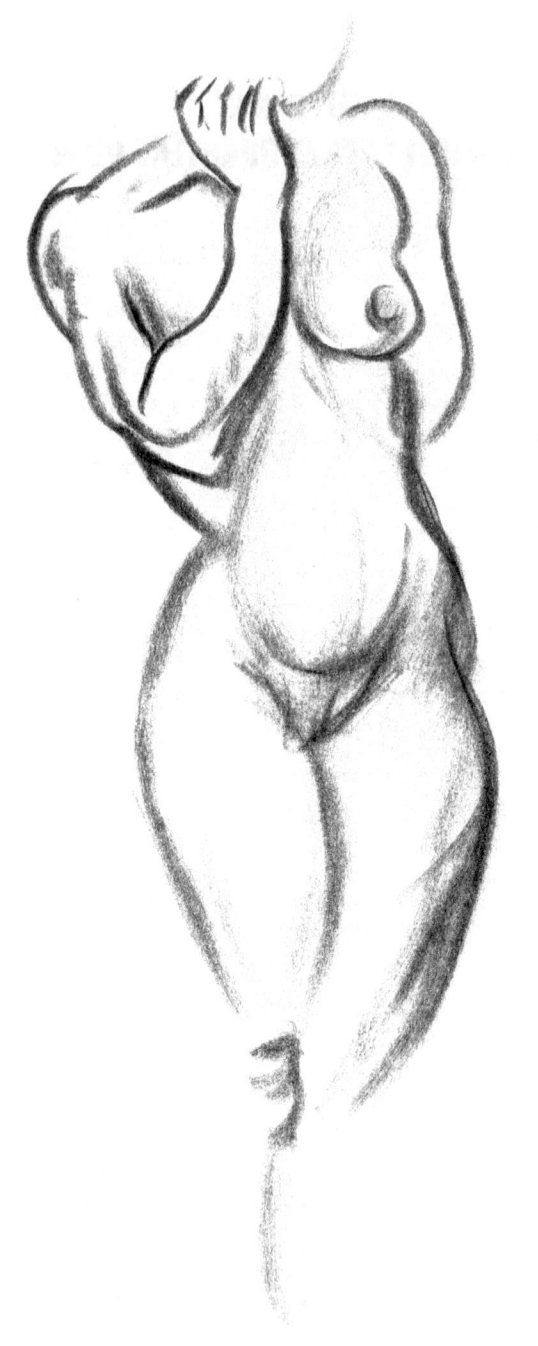

CHAPTER TEN
THE FRONT OF THE FIGURE

The construction lines for the figure, viewed from directly in front, are decidedly different from any that have preceded. Here, one side of the figure is convex, while the other is straight. The convex lines appear on the side over the leg that bears the most weight, as the hip on that side is thrust out in order to bring the weight over the center of gravity. When the muscles of the opposite side are relaxed, the hip drops an inch or two and the whole side (not including the small inequalities) assumes the general appearance of a straight line from the armpit to the ankle. When the line of the hips tips one way the line of the shoulders generally tips in the other direction. It can be said, in normal action, that the high hip will be under the low shoulder, and the low hip will be under the high shoulder. It is well to consider the slant of the hips and shoulders, immediately after the construction lines are drawn. The figures in the following four photographs show how the body falls naturally into the pose described.

DIRECTIONS

Draw the straight line first, and then the curve.

Draw the slant line of the hips and shoulders between the two curves at once.

It will be a great assistance in drawing, to remember that the shoulder line always slants down, and that the hip line up, from the straight side; for the action of the front of the figure depends almost as much on the slant lines as on the two long curves.

Draw six figures from casts or pictures. Be careful to make the construction lines as described above.

Draw six figures from a model posing as in Chapter Twenty-Four. Make the construction lines with care, and draw the figure in outline, lightly, before attempting to introduce any drapery.

Draw four figures from memory with the arms of each in different positions.

QUESTIONS: What is the nature of the change in construction in this chapter? Explain how the shoulders and hips slant in opposite directions when the weight is on one foot. Repeat carefully the directions to be given to students beginning this lesson. Can you draw a figure from memory on these construction lines? Had you ever noticed before that the low shoulder came over the high hip? Can you find a picture in which this is not true? Does an exception always prove the rule? Is the rule of construction in Chapter Ten a fairly safe one to follow? Why?

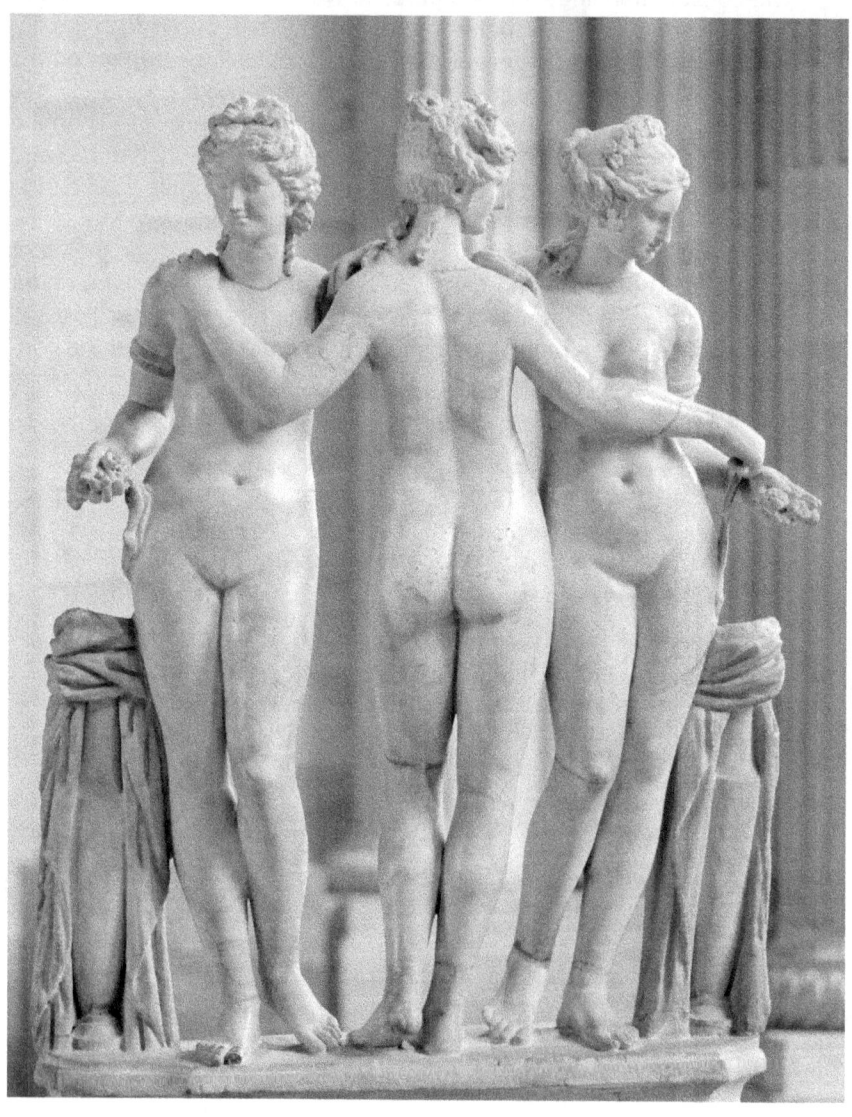

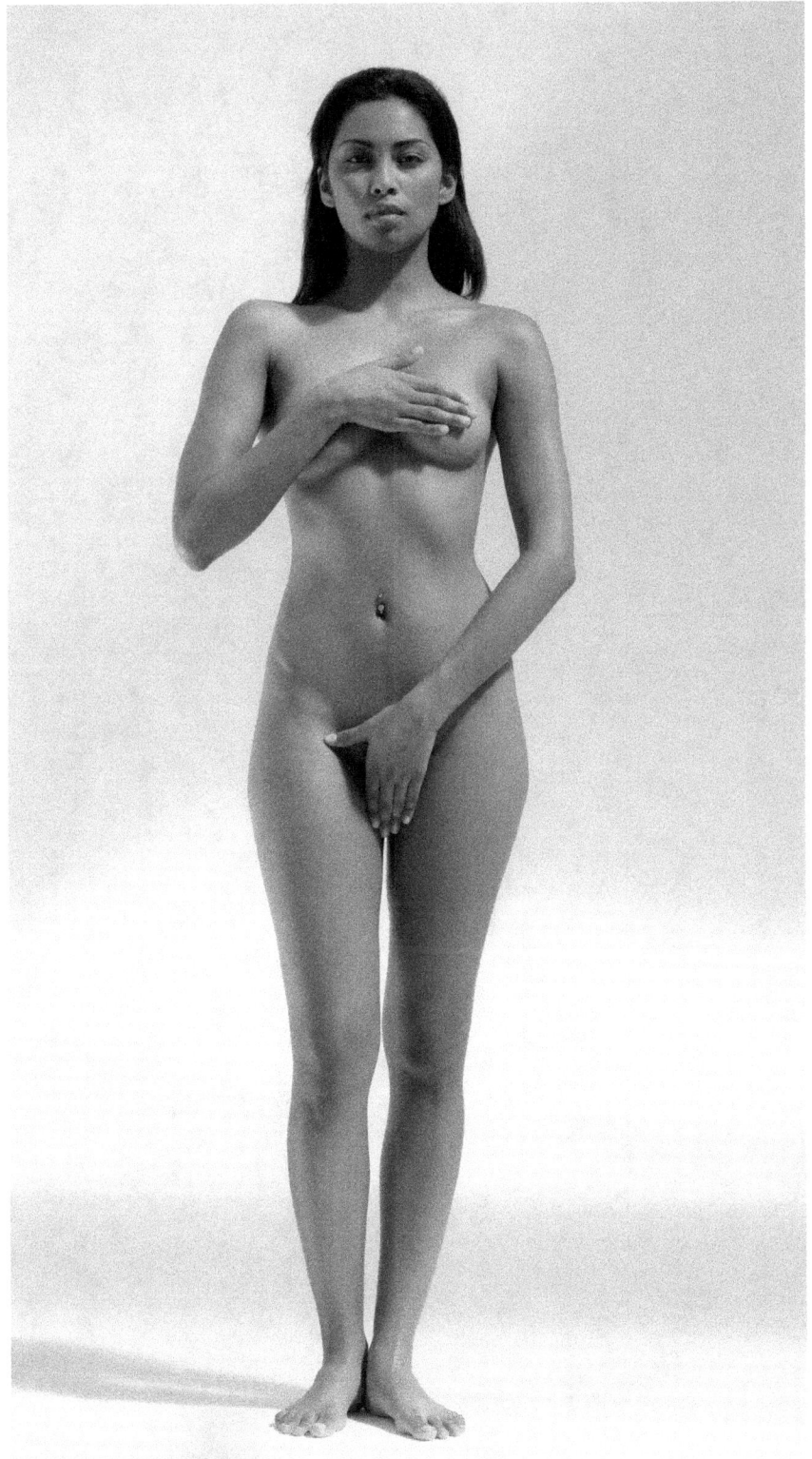

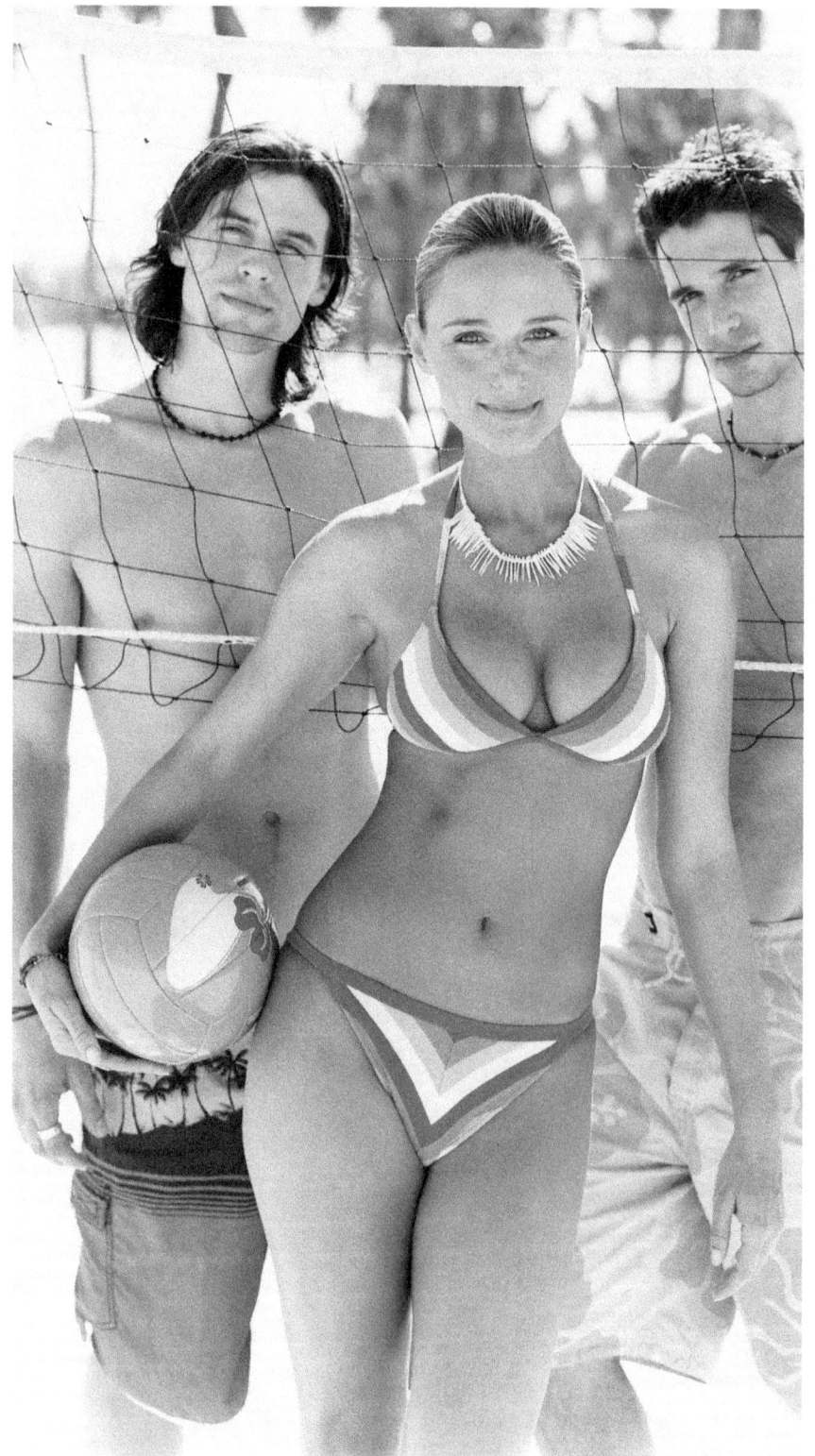

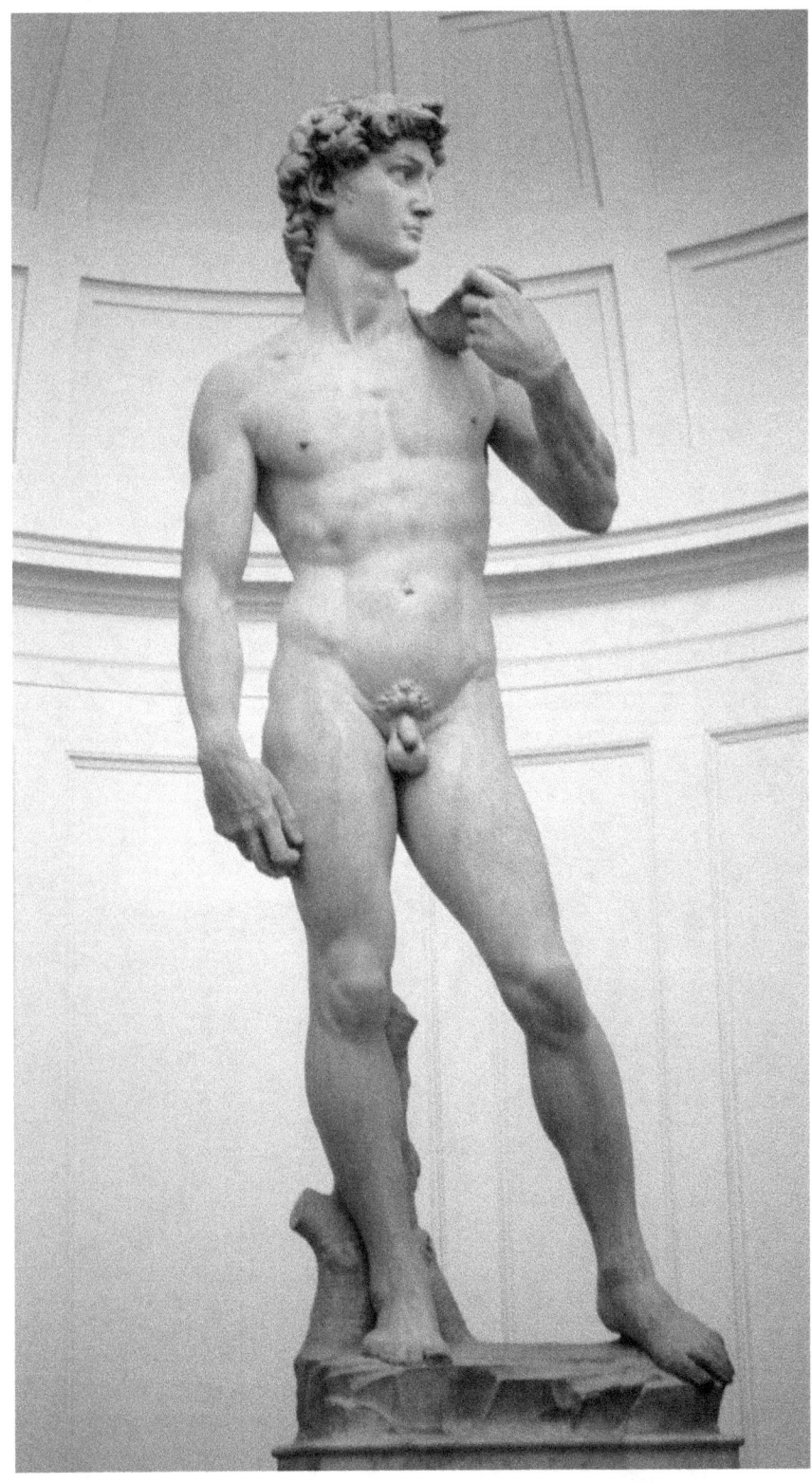

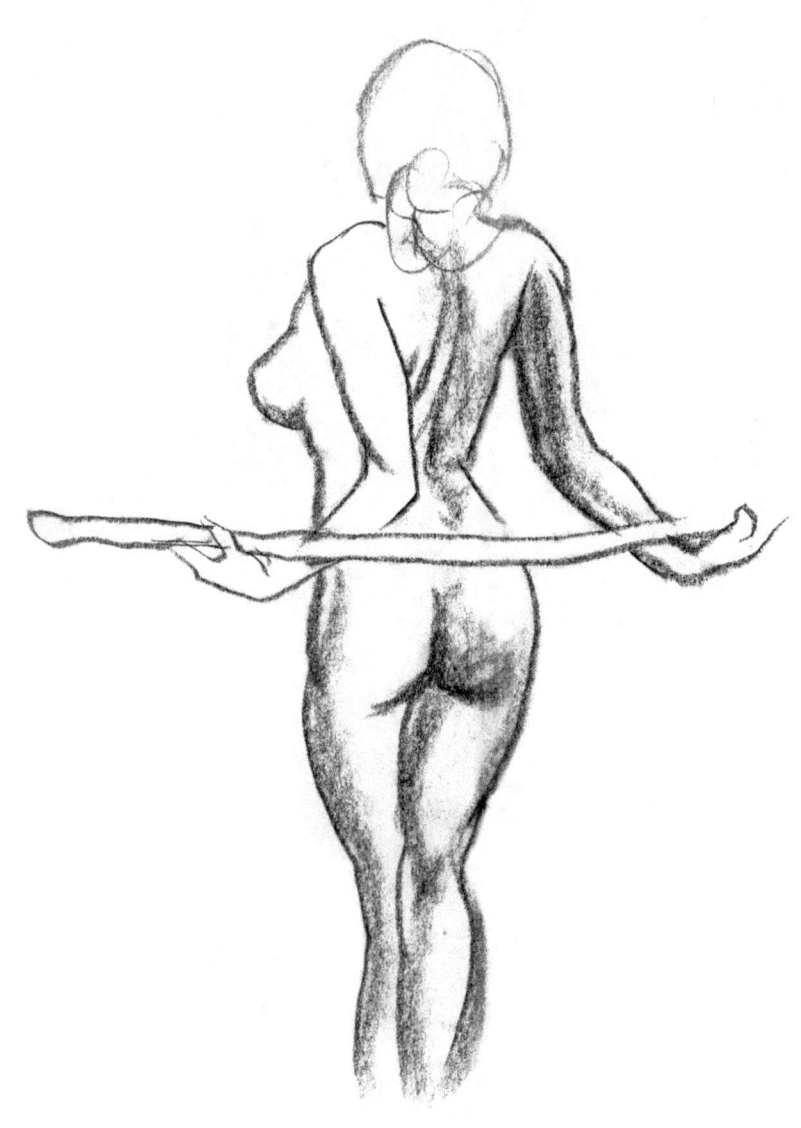

CHAPTER ELEVEN
MEMORY AND IMAGINATION

Drawing from memory is strongly advocated by all teachers of art, both ancient and modern. It strengthens the impressions gained by the study of nature, and stimulates those powers of imagination and invention that every artist must possess in order to produce original works of art.

The composition on the opposite page was made from the directions of the instructor to draw two kneeling figures in decorative costume. The drawing is interesting because each line of the drapery duplicates the concave and convex contours of the figure. It is thus built up from memory on the exact shapes of the figure, and the imagination has supplied the type of drapery and the lines that each is likely to assume when superimposed on the figure.

DIRECTIONS

Draw from memory a figure from any of the previous chapters, in four minutes.

Draw from imagination and memory, after looking once, the figure in Chapter Five, with a few lines for drapery.

Draw a figure that is unlike any shown in the previous chapters, but in which parts of several of them are used.

Draw, in four minutes, two kneeling figures without drapery. In the same manner, draw two with drapery.

Pay especial attention to the kind of technique obtained in this memory drawing, for it is the habit of some students to return to a poor quality of line at this point.

QUESTIONS: What is the difference between drawing from memory and drawing from imagination? How does drawing from memory assist the student? How will drawing from one's imagination assist the student? Have there been artists who have drawn too much from imagination? Explain, if you can, how this could be true. What do you think is the fault most noticeable in many of the fashion drawings?

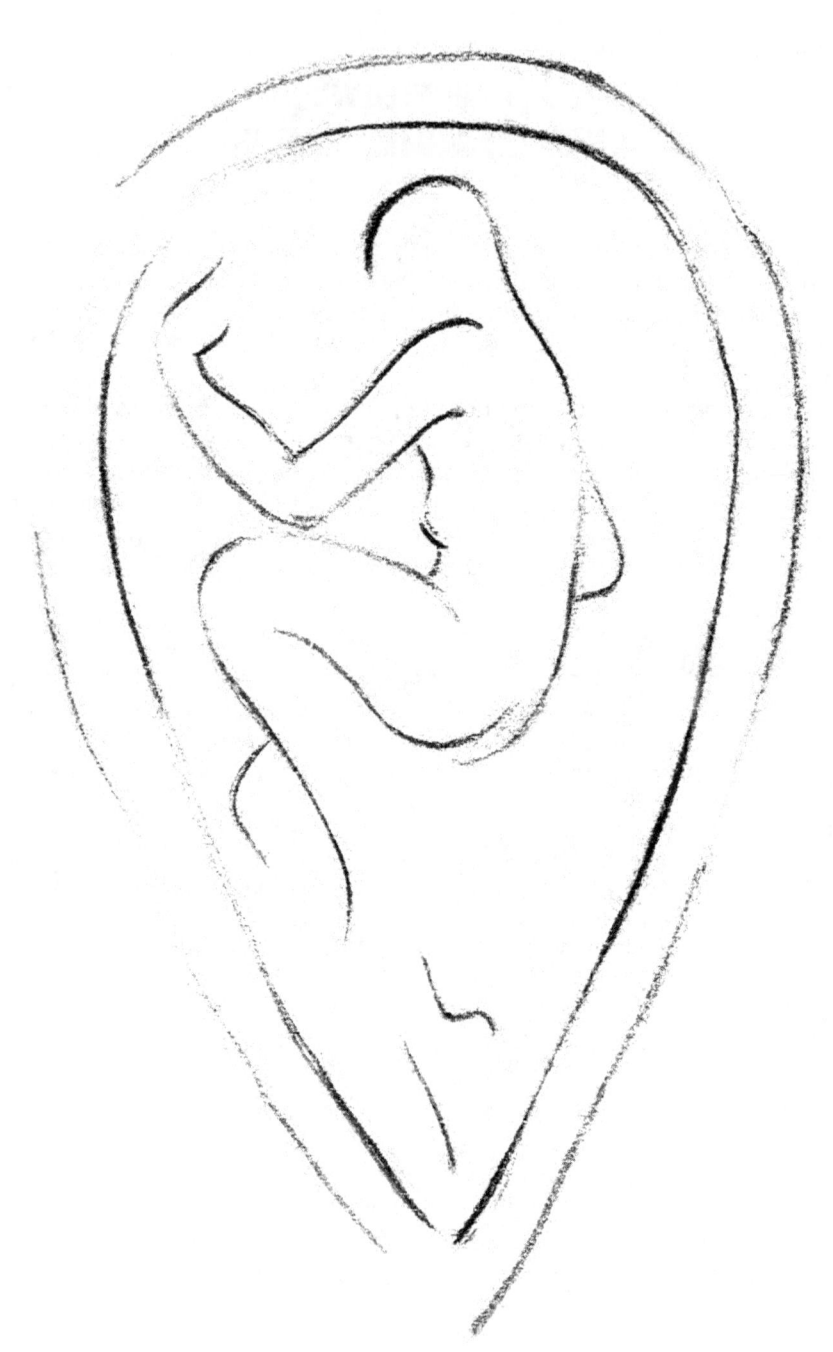

CHAPTER TWELVE
ADAPTABILITY

The human figure, as a decorative motive, has marvelous adaptability. There is hardly a shape into which it will not fit with grace and beauty. A class exercise that demonstrates the ease with which it may be adapted to any arrangement of curved lines is given below.

In the drawing on the left, the form was drawn almost the exact size from a fifteenth century metal shield on which was embossed an ornamental lion. Here the student not only filled the space well, but succeeded in giving to the figure the characteristic lines of the animal that occupied the space.

The Greek Cross (bottom left), a difficult shape to fill on account of the corners, was filled in, in four minutes, by a student with practically no experience, and although the drawing can hardly be said to be good, the space is agreeably filled, and owing to the correct placing of the convex and concave lines on the figure, there is no question of the action the student intended to express.

In the second drawing (bottom right), the figure is again drawn in spaces originally occupied by beasts. The form was taken from a fourteenth century target in the Armory Hall of the Metropolitan Museum, where the class went in search of interesting spaces to fill.

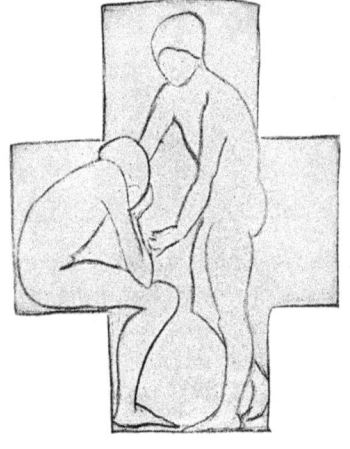

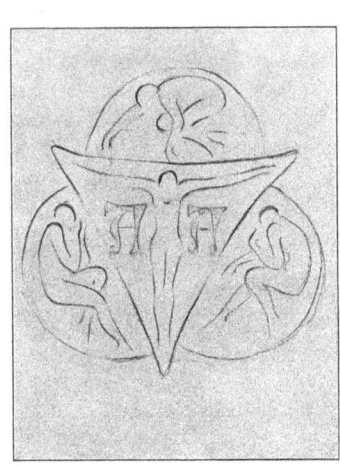

No. 1   **No. 2**

DIRECTIONS

Draw a four-inch square.

Place the curves as in a square, (No. 3), and construct the figure using the long line for the back and the short one for the front of the leg.

Draw a rectangle two inches wide by five inches long.

On the curves shown (No. 4), construct one or two figures (whichever seems most desirable), but be careful to fill the entire space. (Refer to Chapter Seventeen.)

In a four-inch square place two figures built upon curves suggested by another student.

As a final exercise (No. 5), try to fill the spaces suggested in No. 2 with the original figures.

In each case make construction lines.

All drawings should be made in four minutes, excepting that of Plate XII-B. In this two minutes may be permitted for each single figure.

NOTE: The reproduction of a portion of the decoration for the Parthenon gives an idea of the way similar problems were solved by the Greeks. It is interesting to observe that the figures are inscribed in a circular line in which the drapery plays an important part.

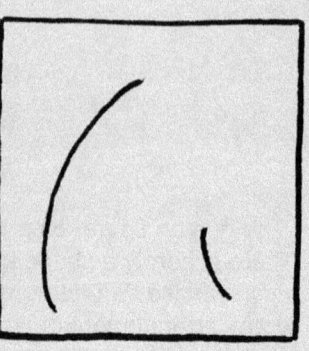

No. 3

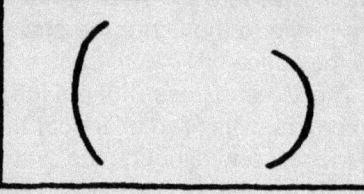

No. 4

No. 5

QUESTIONS: *Is the human figure especially adaptable as a decorative motive? What qualities make it so? Explain how drawing the figure on prescribed lines inside the limit of a square is instructive. Does the use of more than one figure make the filling of a space easier or more difficult? Why did all the great masters use the figure so continually for decorative purposes? Was it because the figure is especially easy to draw in a space, or was it because it is especially fitting to use the figure in decoration? Are the greatest decorations in the world figures? Name one.*

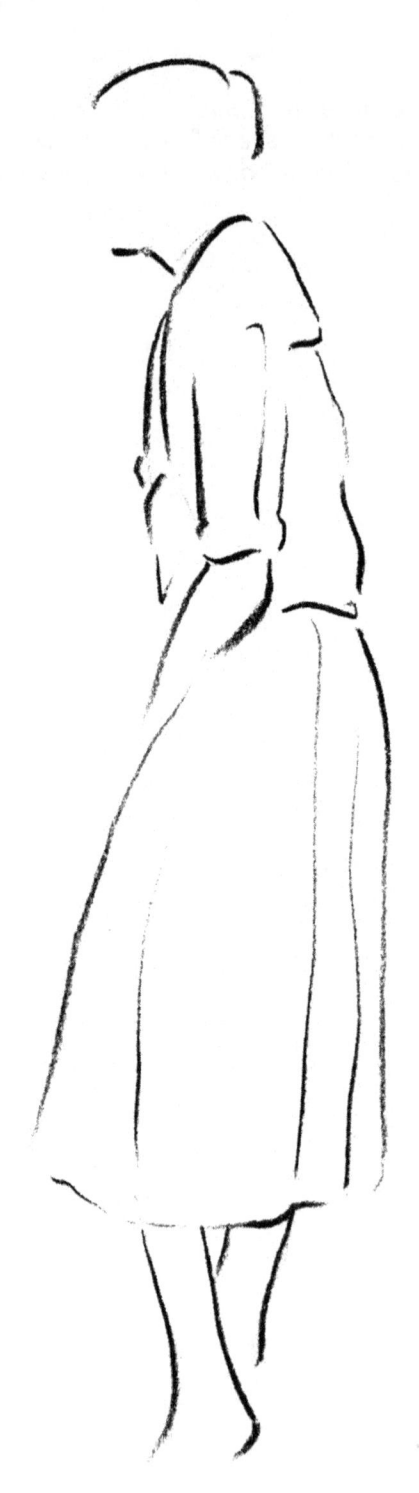

CHAPTER THIRTEEN
THE DOUBLE CURVE

The first real change in construction lines came in Chapter Ten, when a straight line was used with a convex line instead of the usual concave curve. In this chapter both construction lines are new. The figure is bent forward from the hips in such a manner that the upper part of the usually concave line of the back is convex. The whole line of the back including the legs is a double curve, as is also the front line.

The action of the figure seems to be the most clearly expressed by drawing only the convex parts of the double curves as in the diagram shown below.

DIRECTIONS

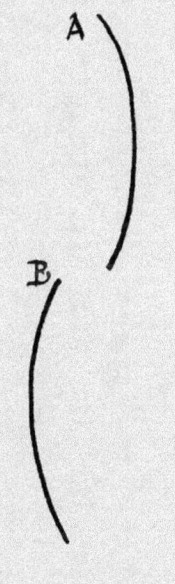

Draw the construction lines A and B, and on a very pale outline of the figure, draw the costume shown in the sketch on the left.

Repeat the exercise five times. Make third and fourth outlines from memory.

Look at the image on page 45. It is an excellent example of the construction lines. Draw it four times from memory, without looking back at the image.

Draw from a pose (one of the students) five or six times. Make the construction lines each time. Use a different pencil with every third or fourth drawing. Use a different paper every second drawing.

QUESTIONS: How does this figure differ in construction from the figure in Chapter One? How does it differ in construction from Chapter Ten? Why is it better to change pencils and paper so often? Can you draw more easily from imagination than from the figure or from the print? Did the great artists of the past recommend drawing from memory? If you were a teacher how much would you allow students to "make up" figures?

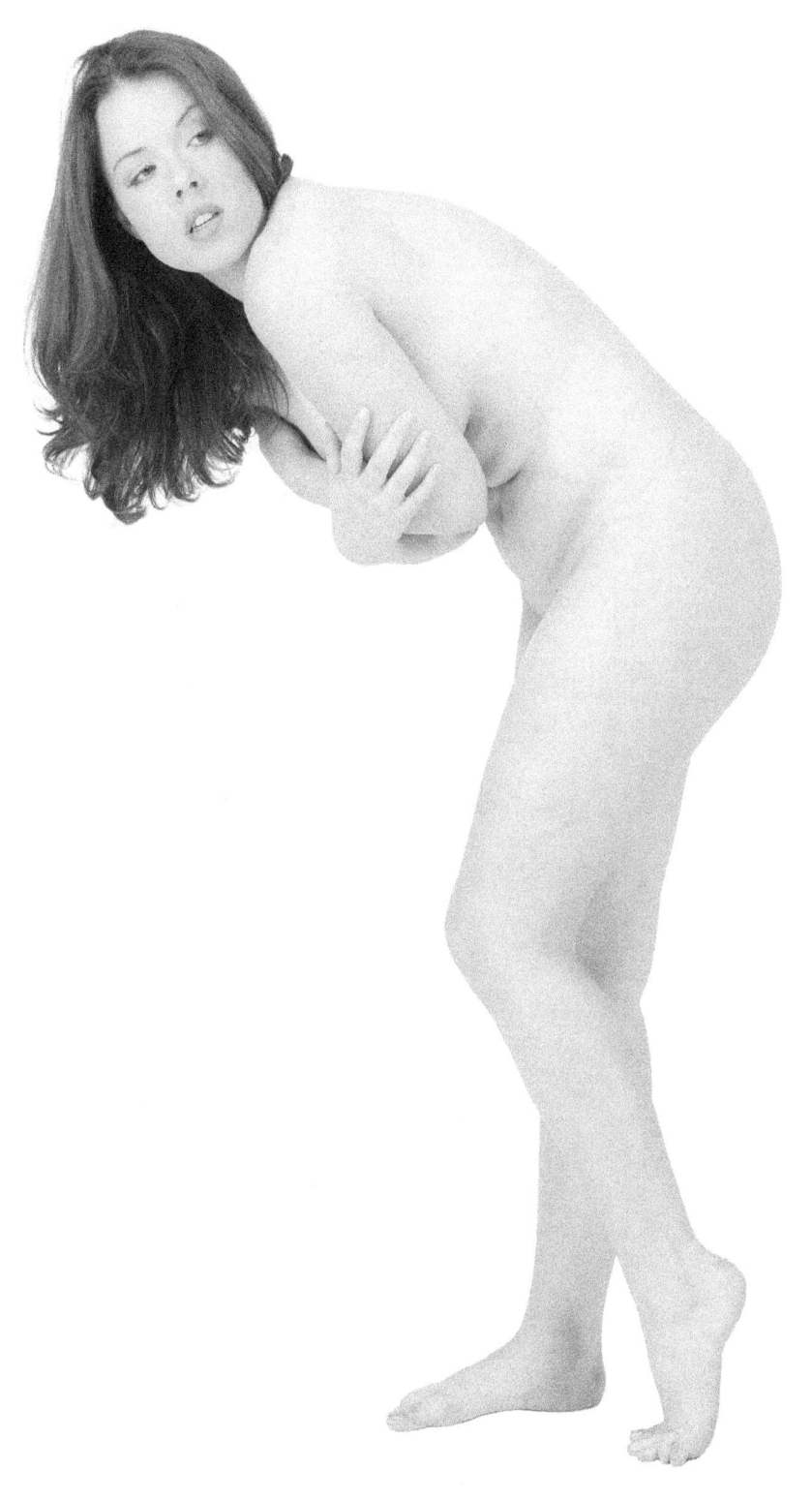

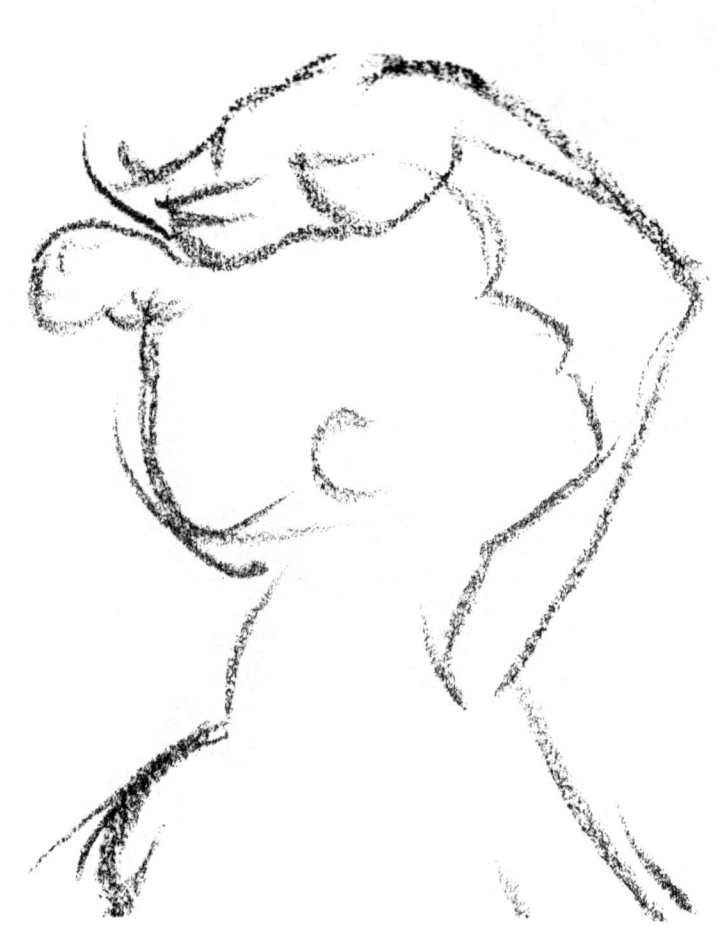

CHAPTER FOURTEEN
THE EAR AS PIVOT

If the ear is well placed there is rarely any difficulty in connecting the head with the rest of the body, for it is easy to imagine that all the lines that do not follow the curves of the outside of the head pass inward and terminate at the ear. It is like a railroad center, with numerous tracks running in from all directions.

All lines point toward the ear such as the curve over the back, the curve of the throat, the line of the jaw, the line of the hair at the temple, and sometimes even the lines of the eyelashes, eyebrows, and mouth.

Practically all the best modes of dressing the hair, particularly the Greek, have lines running to the ear as a basis of their decorative design. More than this, the ear is a fixed point, like the hub of a wheel around which revolve the spokes, for, when the head is tipped forward or backward, the ear acts as a pivot. The position varies with the individual, but its lowest point is usually about opposite the base of the nose, and, if of ordinary size, the top is about opposite the eyes, which, as we have said, are always half way up in the whole space of the head.

DIRECTIONS

Draw the construction lines of the square as in Chapter Three, and the lines leading to the ear.

Draw from a pose (by student) the head in each of the positions on page 49.

Draw the head in profile, from photographs of three very noted people. Observe the difference in the position of the ear on the head in each case.

Draw, from memory, the head of someone well known to you. Do not try to draw the features with exactness, but be sure that you get the exact shape of the whole head.

Draw as often as is possible from the heads of people in the streets and on the cars.

Four minutes is long enough for each drawing.

QUESTIONS: Describe how the ear is the pivot on which the head seems to turn. Show in a quick sketch how the lines seem to center on it. What lines do not turn in toward it? Is the ear in the center of the head?

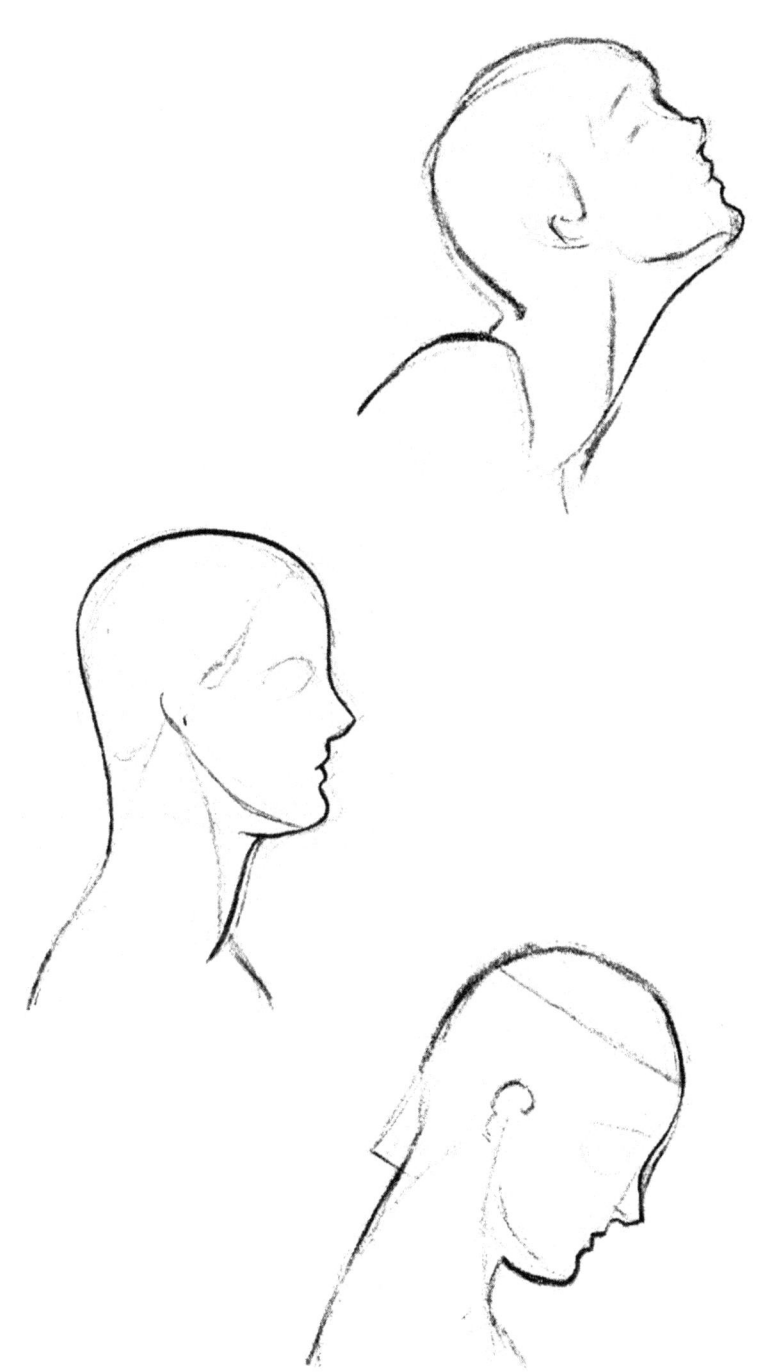

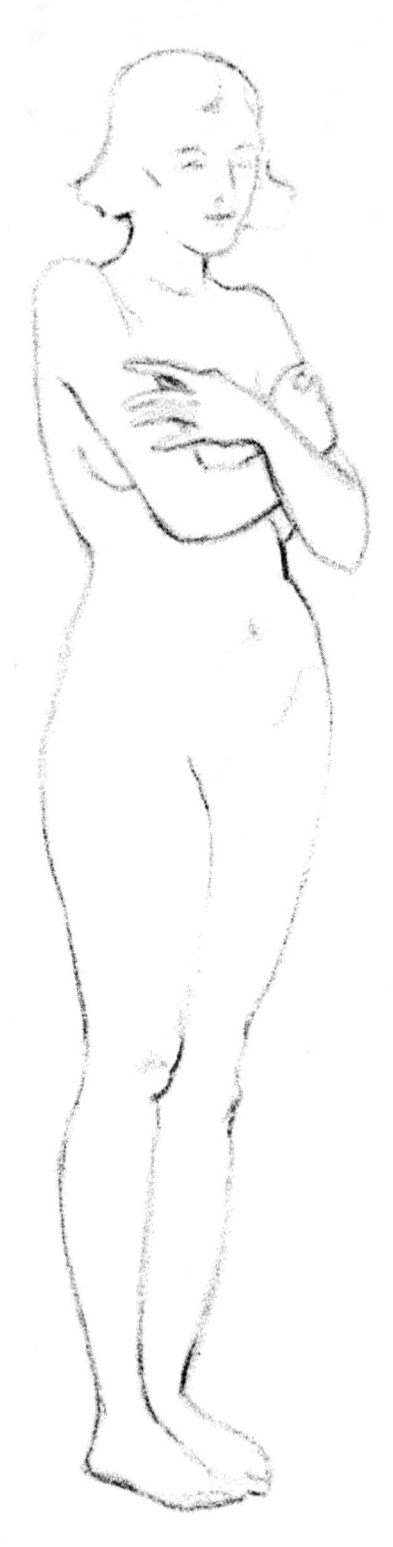

CHAPTER FIFTEEN
THE STANDING FIGURE - THREE-QUARTERS VIEW

The figure (opposite page) is standing on both feet, and would be bisymmetrical if seen from the front. As it is, there is only a slight variation from that position. It is only after close scrutiny that the difference of sides becomes apparent, and the right side is seen to be a convex line, while the left side approaches to a straight one.

A figure in this position is a very difficult one to draw. The construction lines should be made with more care than usual.

This figure was drawn in six and one-half minutes; the extra time of two and one-half minutes was spent in drawing the hands, of which the left one is slightly too large.

DIRECTIONS

Draw the figure carefully in four minutes as it ap-pears on the opposite page, omitting the hands, arms, and features.

Draw the figure facing the opposite direction three times in twelve minutes.

Copy in four minutes the drawing on page 28.

Draw the figure on the opposite page in four minutes, with the arms in another position.

Draw from the imagination a figure that is seen from the three-quarters view. Make its construction lines for the front view.

QUESTIONS: When is the figure said to be bisymmetrical in appearance? Is the figure easy to draw when both sides are nearly alike? Why? Is a figure that is hard to draw necessarily more beautiful than one that is easy to draw? What do you think are the essential qualities of beauty in the figure?

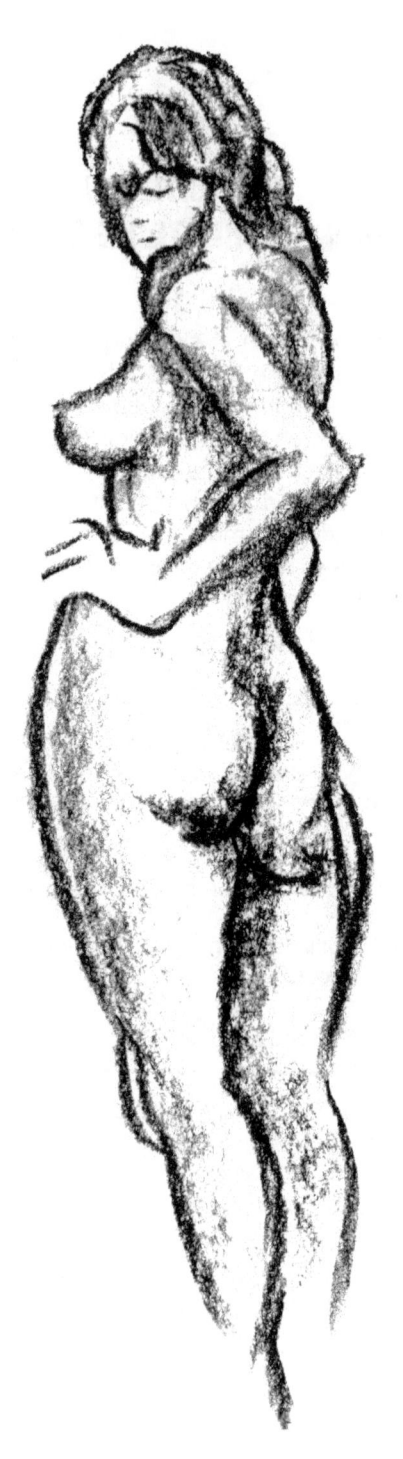

CHAPTER SIXTEEN
TWO CONVEX SIDES

This is one of the few positions of the body in which both construction lines are convex without being bisymmetrical. It contradicts our premise that the figure has a convex and a concave side when not seen from the front. It is an exception that proves the rule.

It is interesting to observe how well the action of the head is supplemented by the strong line of the neck. While the figure is well and solidly placed on its feet, it seems in the act of taking a step to the left. This quality was acquired by a very delicate sense of balance on the part of the artist.

DIRECTIONS

Draw three figures in this position as they would seem to you without drapery.

Draw three more with drapery of a different style.

Draw the head twice in this position; the head and shoulders twice facing the other way. Be sure to keep the relative height of the shoulders exact, as the action of the head depends upon them, as well as upon the neck.

Draw from memory a figure that has, for construction lines, a convex curve and a straight line.

QUESTIONS: Explain just how the construction lines of the figure seem to contradict all the foregoing rules. What is especially well drawn in this figure? Is the figure short-waisted, or does the costume make it so? Is the figure hard or easy to draw compared with the other figures? Is the action simple and easy to understand, or rather complicated? Explain what causes it to be complicated?

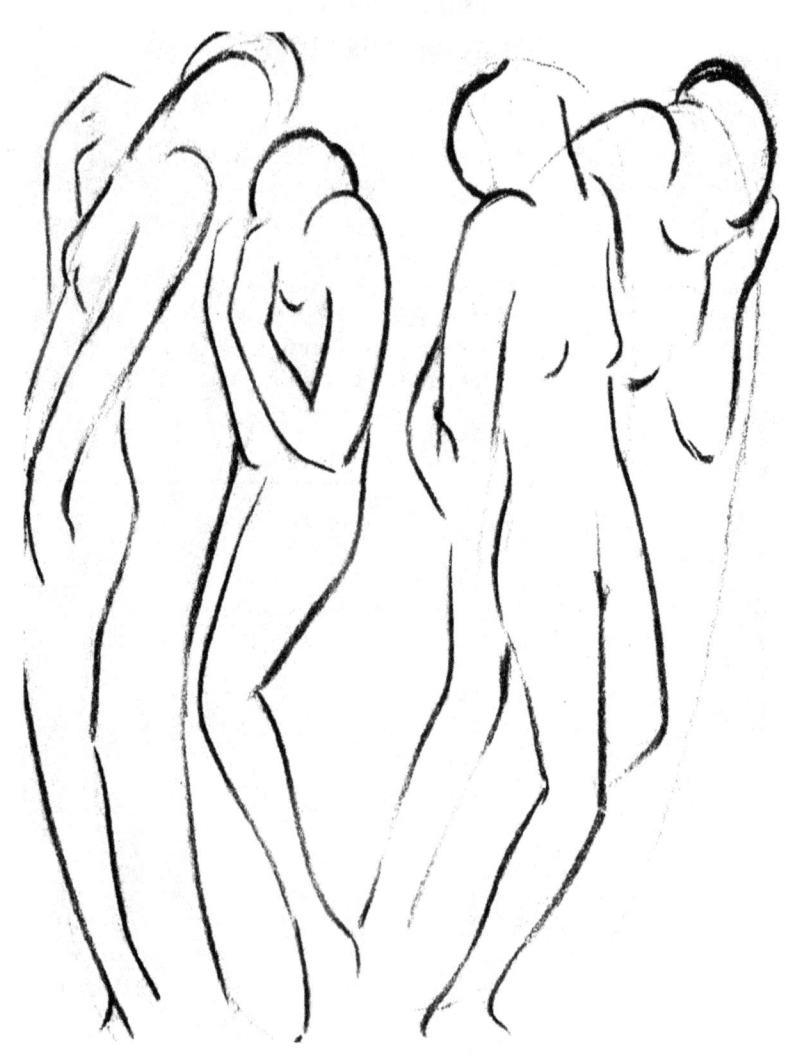

CHAPTER SEVENTEEN
ADAPTABILITY

The combination of figures in the drawing on the left is the result of inscribing in a rectangle a series of loops. The main lines of all the figures except one are drawn exactly on the original curves. In the one exception, the second figure from the right, the curve crosses the body, touches on the outer margin at both sides, and marks the contour as well as the position of the head. A close scrutiny will reveal the original structural lines crossing and recrossing the figures.

The drawing was made with great ease and skill, well within the time limit of four minutes by a first year student. It seems to prove that even in the hands of a beginner the supposedly difficult figure can be handled with great rapidity and with a pleasing result, if the forms are conceived without fear and if the mind is kept keenly alert to its marvelous possibilities.

DIRECTIONS

Draw a square five inches wide and inscribe loops in it as is done in construction drawing. Try to fit in as many figures on these lines as possible in four minutes.

Repeat the exercise using rectangles of different slope. Do not try to complete any of the figures drawn in this way. If the composition justifies doing so, copy it on another sheet and in that way insure the protection of the first spontaneous sketch.

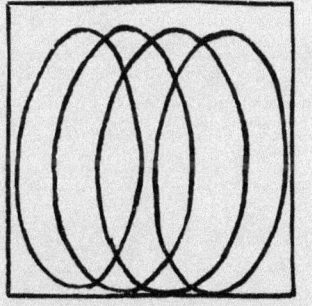

NOTE: It is in this lesson that the student should attain his or her ultimate speed and for the moment relinquish all attention to measurement and proportion, simply working for decorative forms and speed.

QUESTIONS: Describe the process employed in drawing the group figure in the image on the left. Give reasons why imagination is a necessary attribute in this kind of drawing. Does it give the student a sense of power to draw rapidly? Why is drawing done too slowly apt to harm the composition?

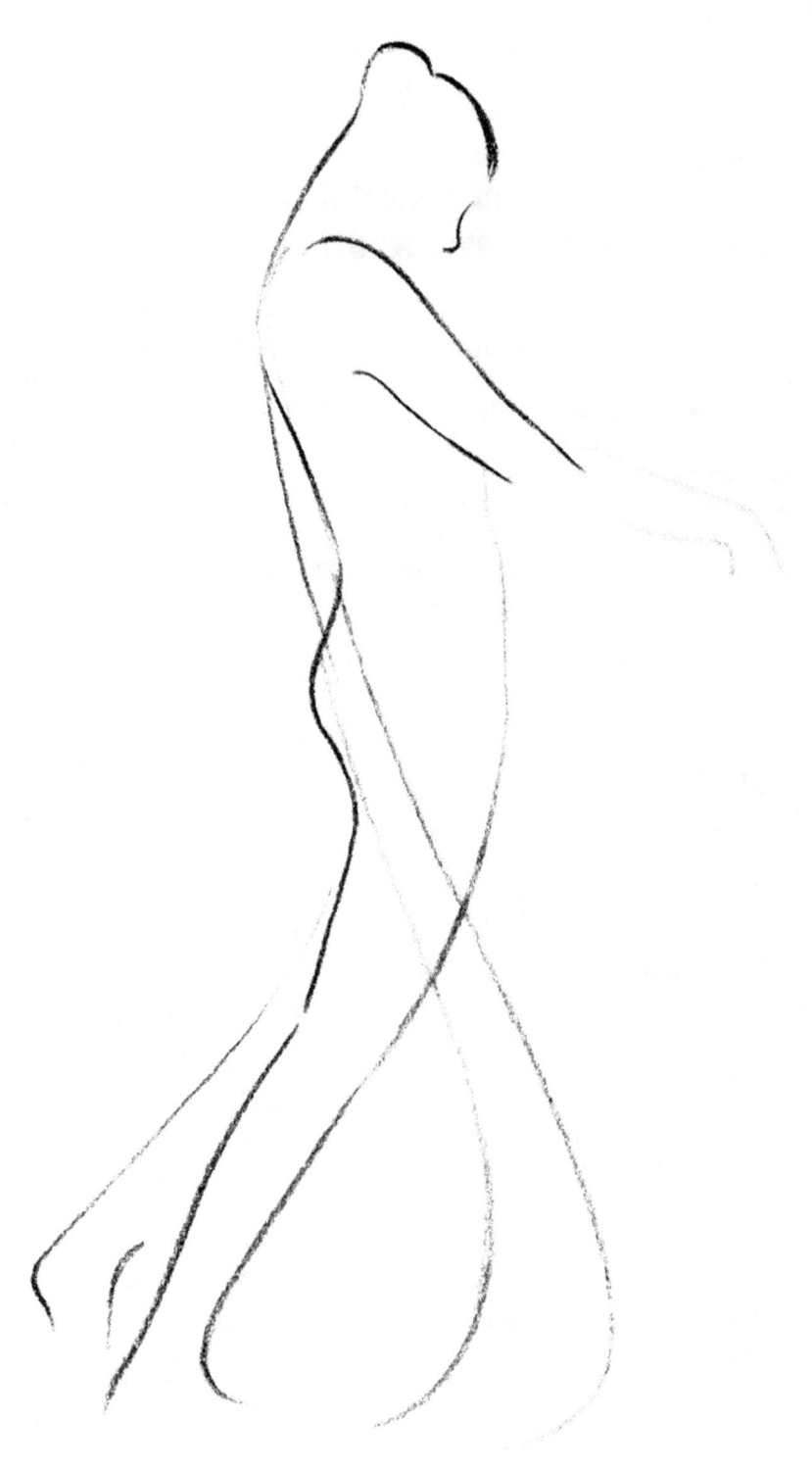

CHAPTER EIGHTEEN
THE FIGURE AND LINE

In Chapter Eighteen the construction lines are those of Chapter One. The new and distinctive feature in this chapter is the manner in which the decorative lines of the drapery are suggested in relation to the lines of the figure.

Many races have tried to enhance the figure by adding costume or drapery to it. It remained for the Greeks to do it most perfectly, for they had especial appreciation and reverence for the figure itself, and they followed its lines whenever possible. The Japanese have splendid appreciation for design and texture, but in costume their surface pattern as well as the shape of the garment, is often used in such a way as to draw the attention away from the lines of the figure rather than to it.

In this figure it is interesting to note that the construction lines at the front and back seem to be bent at the end in such a manner that the whole line suggests a double curve or the letter S9 and that these curves have the effect of carrying the eye back toward the center.

Opposed to these are two lines of drapery that have very much the same character except that they are reversed. Taken together they make a very harmonious whole and form a series of paths that is very easy for the eye to follow; thus, aside from any meaning that the lines may have, the psychological pleasure of following them is so great that the observer is continually returning to them.

DIRECTIONS

Draw the figure in the image on the left five or six times, attempting to add to the outlines of the contours a feeling for the line that returns on itself.

Draw from memory six or seven figures in different positions. From the main lines of these figures draw lines that will serve as drapery, but will have a true decorative relation to the figure. Draw the lines with freedom, speed, and power.

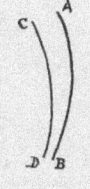

QUESTIONS: What was the artist Hogarth's theory? What interesting power has this line over the eye? Why are the Greeks supreme as costume designers? In what respect do the Japanese seem to fail?

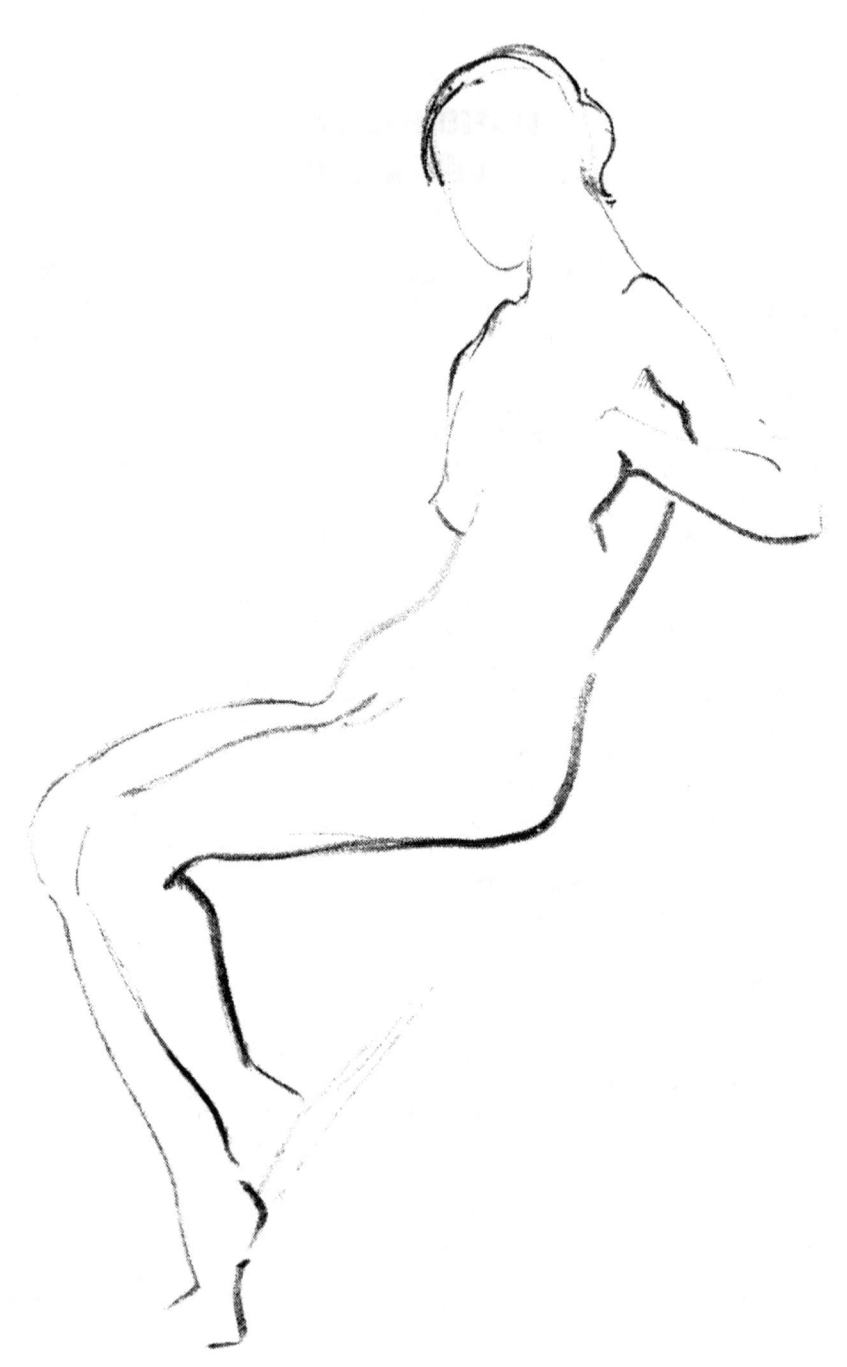

CHAPTER NINETEEN
THE SITTING FIGURE, NO. 1

A sitting figure is considered difficult to draw because of the short lengths into which the long lines are broken. In this apparent confusion, however, there is always a certain structural order that may be based on convex and concave curves.

In this case it is not difficult to imagine one beginning at the base of the skull and extending downward past the shoulders and back of the thighs, and finally to the feet, where it will usually pass directly along the soles of one of them.

The rules for the convex and concave lines in the other parts of the figure hold good in the sitting figure.

In drawing this figure the heavy and light lines were made with the same pencil. It was held nearly flat for the darker ones.

DIRECTIONS

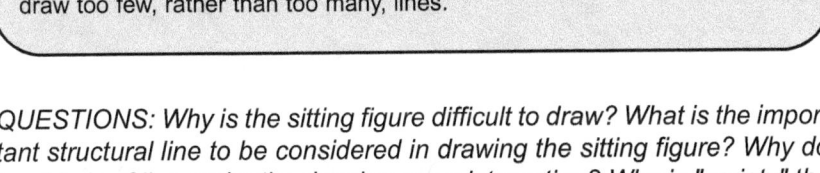

Draw the figure four or five times as it is, without accent on the lines.

Draw it twice with the heavy lines made as shown in the drawing by holding the pencil flat in the hand.

Draw two figures with the accents in new places.

Draw this figure with the suggested drapery used in Chapter Eighteen.

Think carefully where the lines of drapery will best leave the lines of the figure, and then draw each with one clean sweep of the pencil. It is better to draw too few, rather than too many, lines.

QUESTIONS: Why is the sitting figure difficult to draw? What is the important structural line to be considered in drawing the sitting figure? Why do two kinds of line make the drawing more interesting? Why is "variety" the "spice of life"? Why is the drawing in Chapter Five so interesting when the lines are alike over nearly the whole figure? Is there more than one kind of beauty? Which has the figure in Chapter Eighteen?

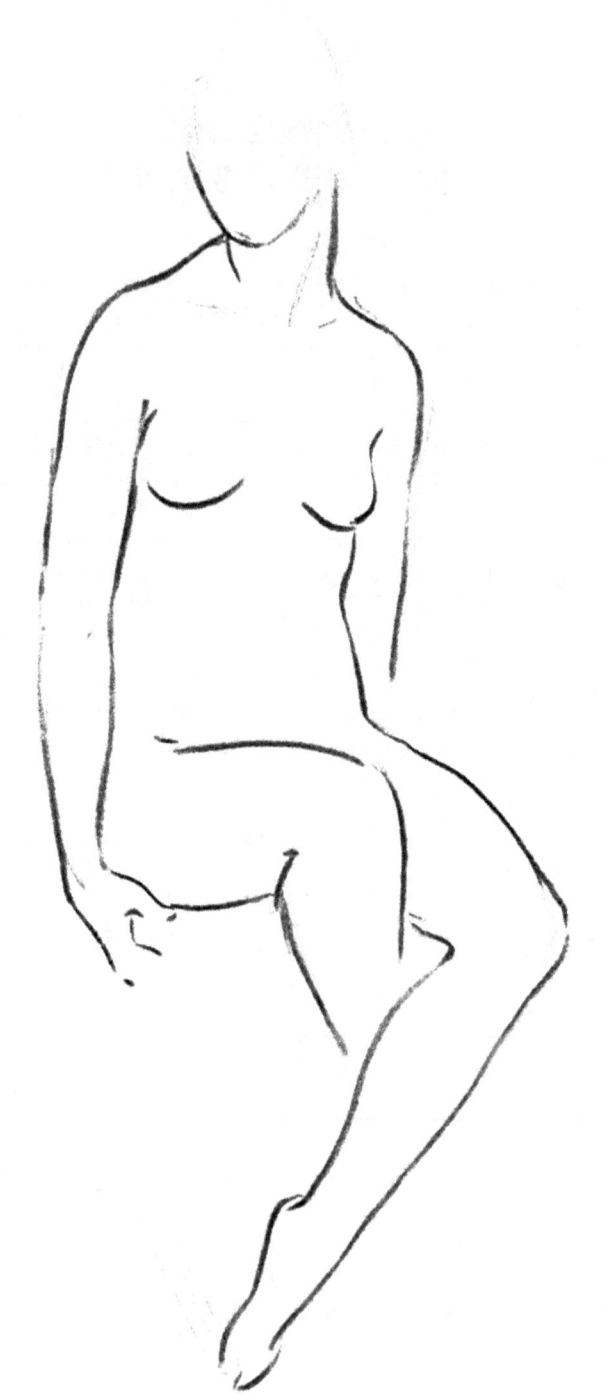

CHAPTER TWENTY
THE SITTING FIGURE, NO. 2

The same line is as important in the three-quarters view as in the true profile. In this case it extends down the arm instead of the side, but it renders the same service as if it went down the side. If it is continued down it extends to the foot, but it reaches the toe rather than the heel.

The more nearly the figure faces the observer, the less likely is the construction line to end exactly in the foot.

In the drawing on the left, if a line be drawn down the right side of the head and neck it will pass, as a double curve, first through the left side at the waist, and then through the inside of the right leg down the left leg to the heel. If this line is not actually drawn as a construction line it should be very carefully studied before beginning the drawing.

DIRECTIONS

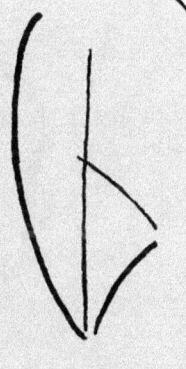

Draw the figure six times, every other time in reverse.

Without looking at it, draw the figure in Chapter Nineteen twice from memory.

Draw the figure with both arms in a different position.

Draw the figure and extend the lines as in Chapter Nineteen.

Draw the figure using hard and soft pencils on the same drawing.

Draw the construction lines very lightly. Make two figures facing each other, with costumes as in Chapter Eleven.

Hold the pencil well back from the end. Do not use the same one many times in succession.

QUESTIONS: How do the construction lines of the three-quarters view differ from those of the true profile? What is the similarity? Why is it better to use several kinds of paper? Can one pencil be made to serve the purpose of two? How? Where should the fingers be placed in relation to the point of the pencil? Why? Why is it better to draw rapidly rather than slowly?

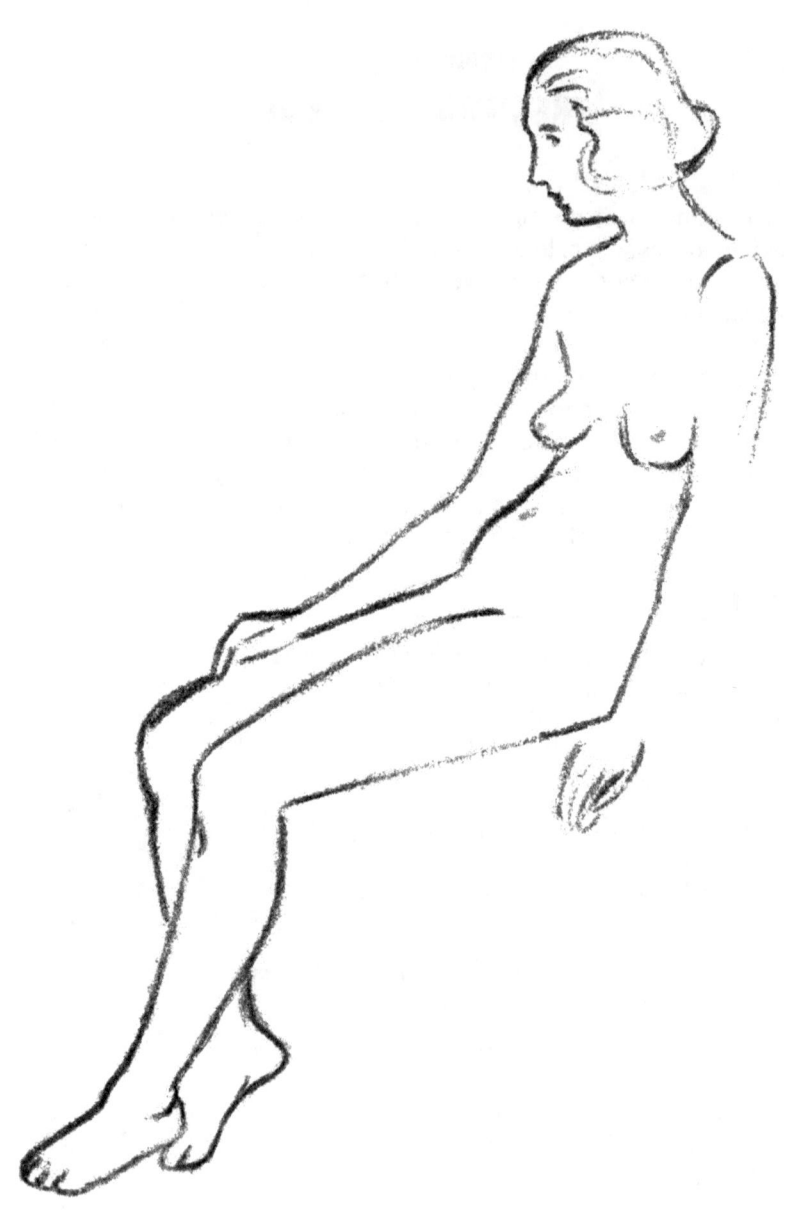

CHAPTER TWENTY-ONE
THE SITTING FIGURE, NO. 3

The construction lines of Chapter Twenty-One are exactly those of Chapter Nineteen, but the figure is handled in a very different manner. The line quality is not nearly as interesting as in Chapter Nineteen, but it is very much more in detail, particularly in the two extremities, the head and feet, the latter being carefully drawn for a short time drawing.

The feet and lower legs are also interesting, on account of the rhythmic quality that appears to connect the line of one with the other. The absence of a line down the arm seems to ameliorate the monotonous quality of the outline.

DIRECTIONS

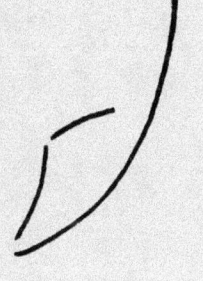

Draw from memory the figure in Chapter Nineteen. Leave out any part of the outline that seems unimportant.

Draw the figure four times, every other time reversed.

Draw it from memory and leave out any part that does not harm the action.

Draw the head, arms, and torso of the figure in Chapter Nine in a sitting position.

In the same manner draw the figure in Chapter Five in a sitting position.

QUESTIONS: With your pencil trace in the air the rhythmic lines in the feet and lower legs of the figure. Is the line quality especially good in this figure? What qualities has it, good or bad? Does the omission of the line of the arm seem to hurt it? Which of the three sitting figures is the most difficult to draw? Why?

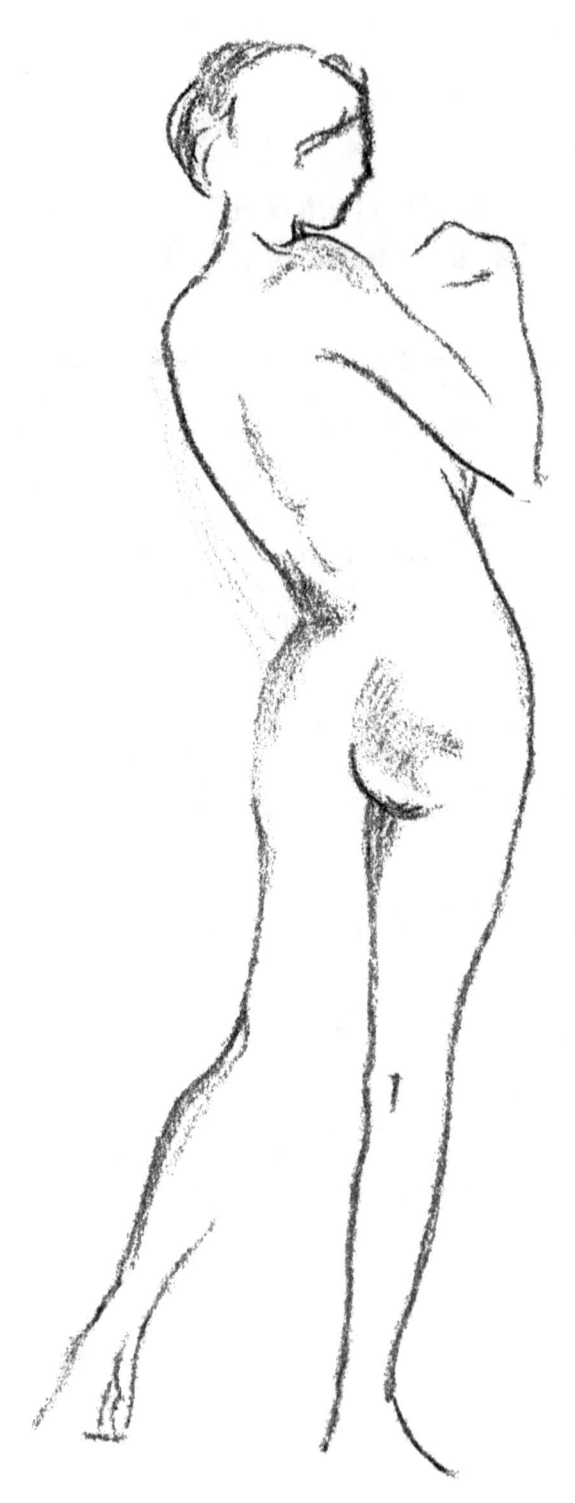

CHAPTER TWENTY-TWO
BEGINNING SHADING

When the figure in action stands with its weight distributed equally on both feet, the student is at liberty to choose the line of action. In the drawing on the left it seems to be the construction line that passes from the shoulder, over the hip, to the ankle. The action of the back may be considered as continuing on down either leg. The twist of the body has drawn the inside muscles of the right leg to a position where they are nearly straight. There is a suggestion of shadow here and there on the figure, drawn, not as an isolated shade, but in connection with the outline.

The student should begin shading by observing each widening of the outline without any attempt at drawing, and should then draw in, with rather pale lines, a few of the most important ones.

DIRECTIONS

Draw in order construction lines A and B. Draw line BC, if it seems more important than D. The head may be expressed by a slightly widened circle.

Pay special attention to the position of the feet—one is higher than the other.

Draw the figure six times in the given position, and then reverse it.

Try to fit a modern dress on a similar figure.

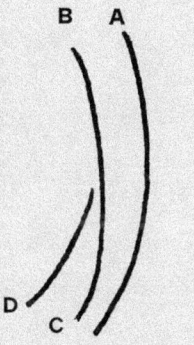

QUESTIONS: When the figure in action stands on both feet, which side has the greater action? Is there any way of telling where the important line will be found? In this case which of the two possible construction lines at the back seems more important? Describe how to begin shading. Where is the unusual line in this figure; that is, the one that seems less well described by the methods explained in Figure Construction?

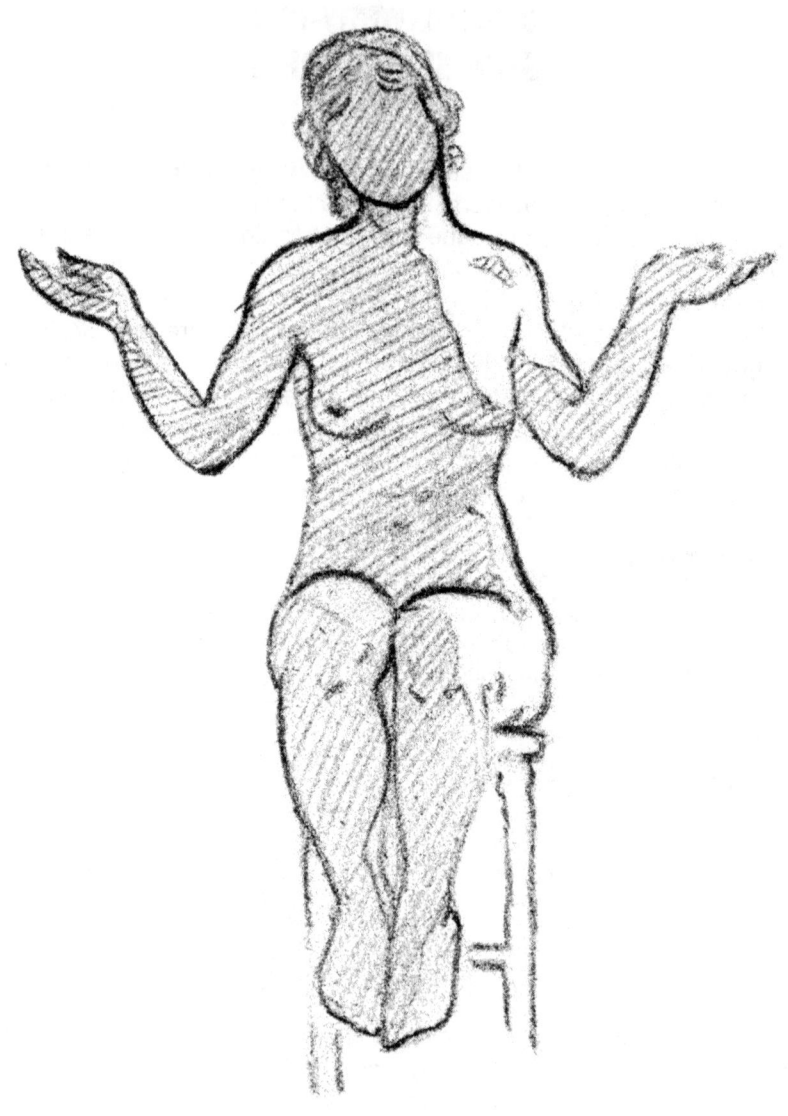

CHAPTER TWENTY-THREE
SYMMETRY

In drawing objects that are alike on both sides it is advisable to draw a vertical line down through the center. By so doing, it is possible to measure the exact width of the opposite sides at any point using the vertical line as a center. In this particular figure there are several departures from true symmetry. A line drawn through the center of the torso would not pass through the center of the head, nor exactly between the feet. In this case and other cases of like character it is well to show the variance from exact symmetry and the center by construction lines as given below.

DIRECTIONS

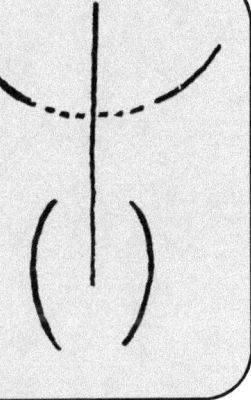

Make construction lines. Draw this figure six times from memory.

Draw it twice with the feet and legs, from the knees down, in a different position.

Try to draw it once with the head straight, above the torso.

Make a design of flowing drapery extending from the shoulders to the ground on each side, but leaving the knees bare.

QUESTIONS: Why is it difficult to draw a figure that has two sides alike? Why is it likely to be uninteresting to make the two sides the same? In nature are two sides often exactly alike? Are the two sides of the human head ever exactly the same? (It is said that they are not except in case of idiocy.) Explain how symmetry is most advantageously used in architecture and design.

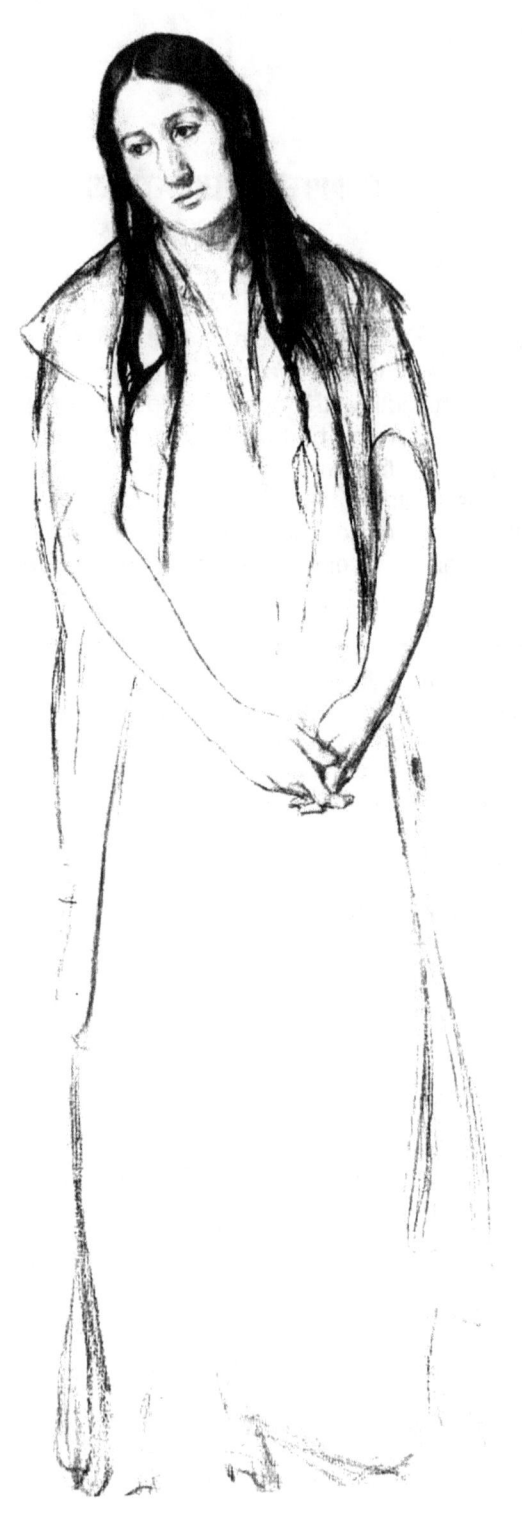

CHAPTER TWENTY-FOUR
CLOTHED FIGURES

This drawing was made from a figure in clothing. The outlines of the figure were drawn partly from what could be seen of it, and partly from memory. The figure on the left was drawn in pale lines, and the clothing, from life, over these lines. A close scrutiny of the drawing will disclose the lines of the figure itself, pale but carefully drawn under the drapery. The feet seem somewhat too large, but the student was not permitted to make any changes after the time expired.

The usual four minutes were allowed for drawing the figure and an additional three minutes for the detail and clothing.

It is better to draw the figure first, because it will give the clothing a much more solid appearance and will prevent any proportions of the body from becoming abnormal. If the artists who draw the fashion designs would adhere to this rule, their drawings would show much more convincingly how the dress would really look when worn by a normal person.

DIRECTIONS

Pose a classmate and draw the pose of the figure in four minutes, and the clothing in three minutes.

Draw the clothing of any figure that you may have before you, in three minutes.

Draw the figure under it in four minutes.

Try to draw the figure under one of the extreme fashion designs. Draw yourself in a mirror.

Make five drawings of a classmate in the position of the figure in Chapter Twenty-Four in the allotted time.

QUESTIONS: Why is it better to draw the figure before putting on the clothing? Do the fashion designs generally show the figure in its true proportions? Is it fair to the public to show clothing on the kind of figure that does not exist? How is this an advantage to the designer? How often do you think the public is deceived by these drawings? If you were buying a dress would you want to see it on a person with a figure like your own, to judge its merits? Will observing so many drawings of improperly proportioned figures make it more difficult for a pupil to learn to draw correctly?

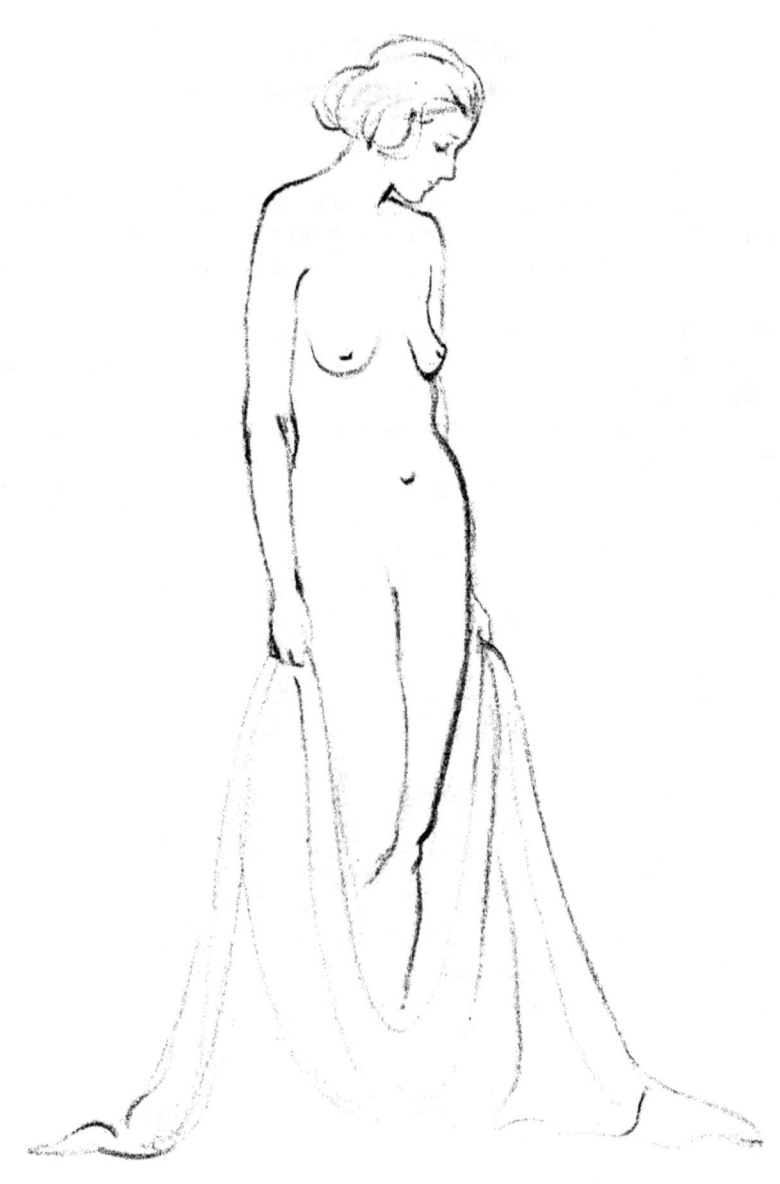

CHAPTER TWENTY-FIVE
FIGURE AND LINE

The construction lines for this chapter are the same as in Chapter One, but the problem is a continuation of the exercises given in Chapter Eighteen. The drapery is drawn in such a manner as to be a continuation of the line of the figure, and shapes the whole into a three-cornered decorative motive. Here the lines do not round back on themselves, as in Chapter Eighteen, except at the very center of the drapery at the bottom, but the ends turn outward and suggest a return outside the picture plane, which, in a way, gives the same result.

DIRECTIONS

Copy the figure on the left twice from memory.

Read carefully the directions given in Chapter Eighteen. Try to draw decorative clothing on the lower part of the figure in Chapter Twenty-One.

Observing that a straight line is the motive, try the same exercise with Chapter Twenty-Six.

NOTE: The drapery should be nearly parallel to the straight line, or should be in opposition to it and parallel to the action of the extended arm.

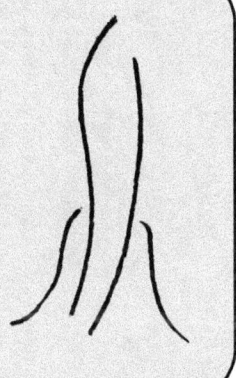

QUESTIONS: Explain why Chapter Eighteen and Chapter Twenty-Five are somewhat similar in intent and purpose. Why are these two chapters important to the costume designer? Why is it easier to make a design with two of the figures in Chapter Twenty-Five than with one? If a costume were designed for the figure in Chapter Six, would it improve or weaken the action? Why? Is the drapery in the image on the left conceived in the manner spoken of above? What figure in this book would you personally like best to design a costume for? Why?

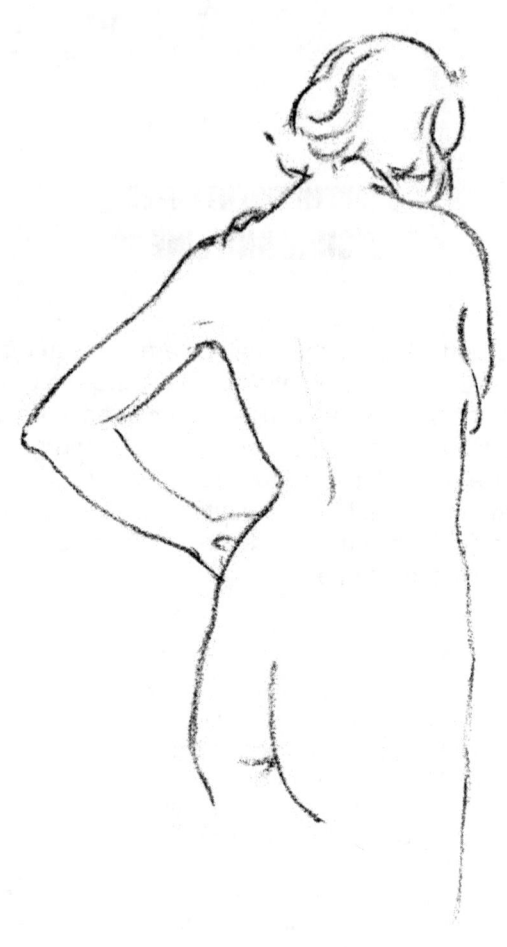

CHAPTER TWENTY-SIX
ABSENCE OF LINE

In nature there is no such thing as *line* in the true sense of the word. *Line* is an invention of man designed to take the place of *edge*. No matter how clearly defined an object may be against its background, there are always some spaces on the edge that are more difficult to see than others.

These are the places on a line drawing where there is least necessity for representation by line. If a line is drawn around an entire figure, it becomes a pattern. It is only by the skillful use of light and dark lines, and here and there the absence of them, that the figure is made to seem round, and to have weight.

It is one of the most difficult things to know when not to draw a line, but a close study of the drawings of the old masters will help, and, gradually, experience will show when the movement and the rhythm of the body is least affected by leaving them off.

In the drawing on the left, the outside of the uplifted arm is left off, yet it is not noticeable, unless the drawing be carefully studied. The absence probably improves the action of the figure.

A drawing must have a synthetic quality and a power of suggestion to seem complete without being finished.

In this particular exercise, the lines have been so cleverly discontinued that the observer supplies the lines for himself, and the figure seems complete, not a fragment as it really is.

DIRECTIONS

Draw several figures in different positions, attempting to discontinue the lines in such a manner that the parts left off will not be missed.

QUESTIONS: Some drawings give the right impression when left incomplete. Others do not. What quality must a drawing have to seem complete when left unfinished? Is line then a convention? Explain how this is true. Give a general rule for the placing of dark and light lines on the figure. Is it easier to know when to draw, or when not to draw a line?

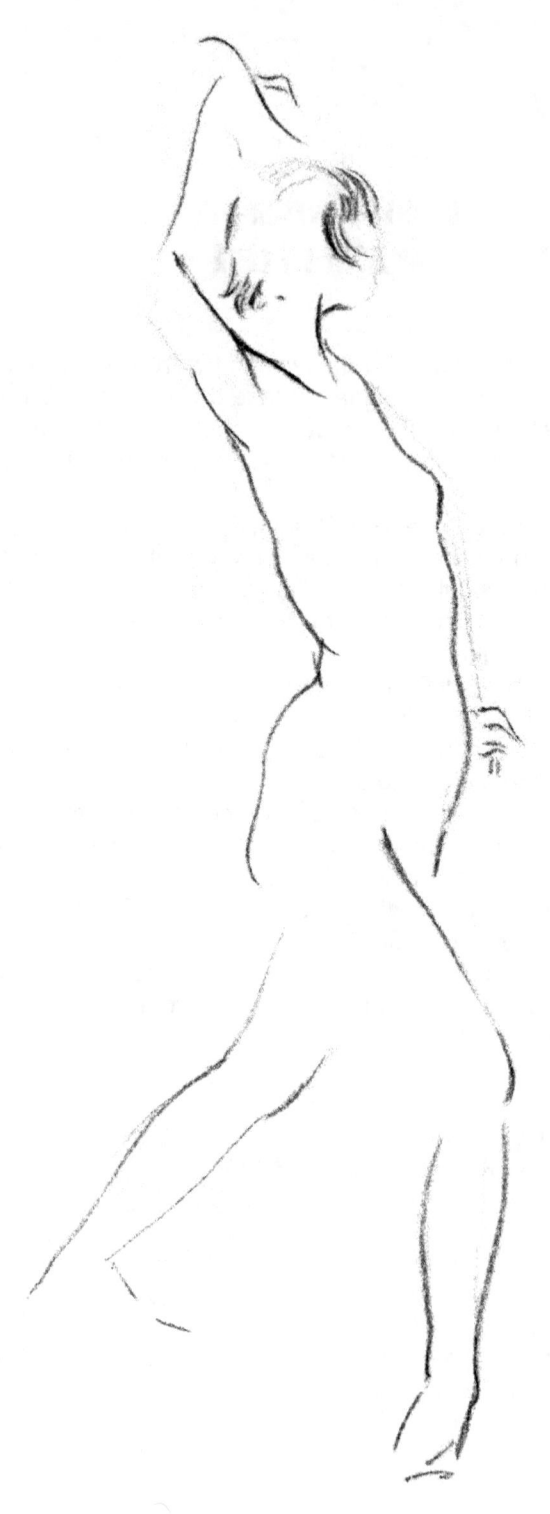

CHAPTER TWENTY-SEVEN
EXTREME ACTION

If the figure in action has its weight distributed equally on both feet the student should choose the construction line that is most obvious. In this case it is the line from the left shoulder to the left ankle.

This is, beyond question, the simplest line of action, although it is not difficult to imagine another line beginning at the same place, bridging the open space from the abdomen to the knees, and extending down to the ankle. Another may be found beginning at the upraised right hand and passing down the inside of the forearm to the outside of the upper arm and side, to the front of the right thigh down to the foot. But the first line is by far the easiest to use because it may be supplemented by the usual concave line at the back.

The relative height of the feet should be very carefully studied. Failure to place them correctly in relation to each other will change the perspective, and will partially destroy the action.

DIRECTIONS

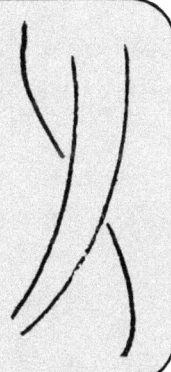

Draw the figure on the left twice as it is.

Draw twice on the same construction line, but change the action of the right leg. It will be seen that without changing the upper part it is difficult to make any change in the right leg that will not injure the appearance of the whole figure.

Draw the figure with both arms and the right leg changed.

On the drawings that have been made try to find a line that may be erased without affecting the action of the whole figure.

QUESTIONS: Describe three lines of action in this figure. Which is the most easily understood of the three? Why is the position of the feet in relation to each other important in all drawings? Does this figure lack the dignity of the one in Chapter VI? Why? Explain how the absence of the line on the upraised arm seems to add to the rhythm of the figure.

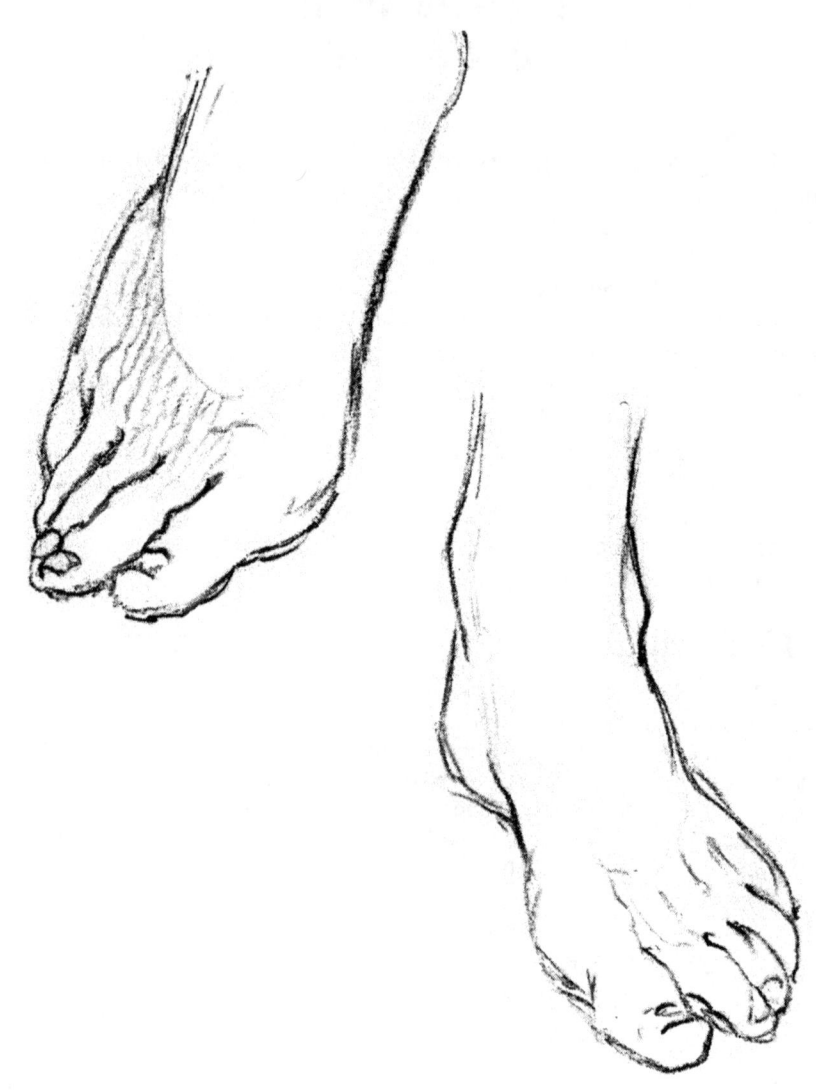

CHAPTER TWENTY-EIGHT
THE FOOT

The foot is comparatively easy to draw when viewed from the side. It may be said to fit into a right angle, the back of the ankle being on the vertical line, the heel slightly outside the vertical line. The sole of the foot, extending along the base may be said to fit into the convex and concave lines used for the figure, the instep being represented by the concave, and the flat of the foot by the convex line. Either of these plans will serve the purpose, but the use of both will give a very clear idea of the character of the whole shape of the foot.

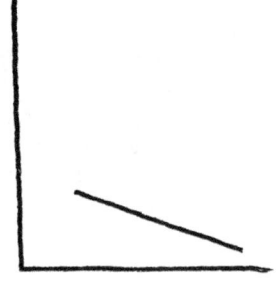

The real difficulty comes when the foot is turned toward the observer and the perspective must be considered. The straight line at the base is used again, but it is no longer horizontal and its inclination must be very carefully considered, as it is this slant of the foot that most surely fixes the position of the figure in relation to its observer. If the angle is wrong, even though the rest of the figure be perfectly drawn, the whole will appear to be weak and unbalanced.

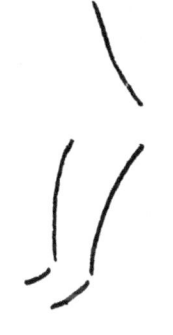

On the shoe a straight line is used, but, in this case, it extends from the bottom of the heel through the ball of the foot, rather than from the place where the heel rests in the shoe.

When the foot is in the position of the one on the left of the accompanying drawing, its structure is expressed by a concave line on the inside, and a convex line on the outside.

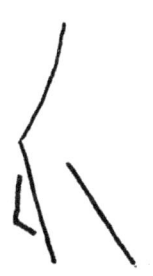

In the foot at the right, the construction is a straight line on the inside, and a convex line on the outside.

From the front of the shinbone an out curve is always found that ends at the ankle. On this curve the inside and outside of the calf of the leg may easily be constructed, and the lines of the foot will follow this curve with exactness.

DIRECTIONS

Draw from memory a shinbone with the out curve. Separate it into two lines at the ankle and extend these lines in a convex and a concave curve down the foot. It will assure the proper attachment to the leg.

Sit in a circle in the classroom and draw in pairs the feet of the students opposite. (If there is a slightly raised model stand to place them on, it will be more in-structive.)

Draw two pairs of feet that toe in.

Draw two pairs that are held very close together, as in Chapter Fifteen.

Draw as many kinds of shoes as it is possible to obtain, from the newest to the oldest and most dilapidated.

Be sure to draw construction lines for each foot.

Two minutes is long enough time for drawing each foot, unless it is shaded.

QUESTIONS: Why is the side view of the foot easy to draw? Why is it difficult to draw from the front? Why is it especially important that the base line be exactly correct as to slant? Illustrate. What is the shape of the shinbone seen from the front? Explain how this characteristic may be useful in attaching the foot to the ankle and leg. Why will an empty shoe help one to learn to draw feet? Which are easier to draw, feet or hands?

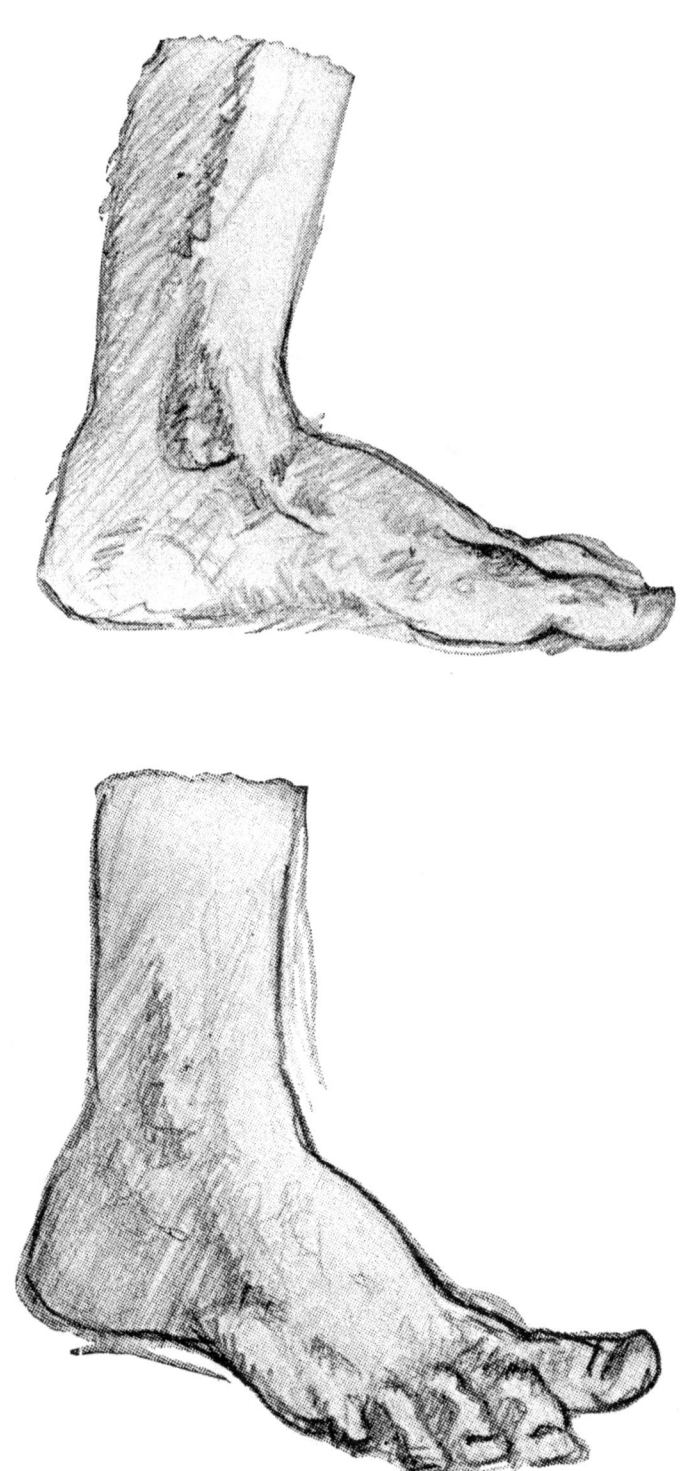

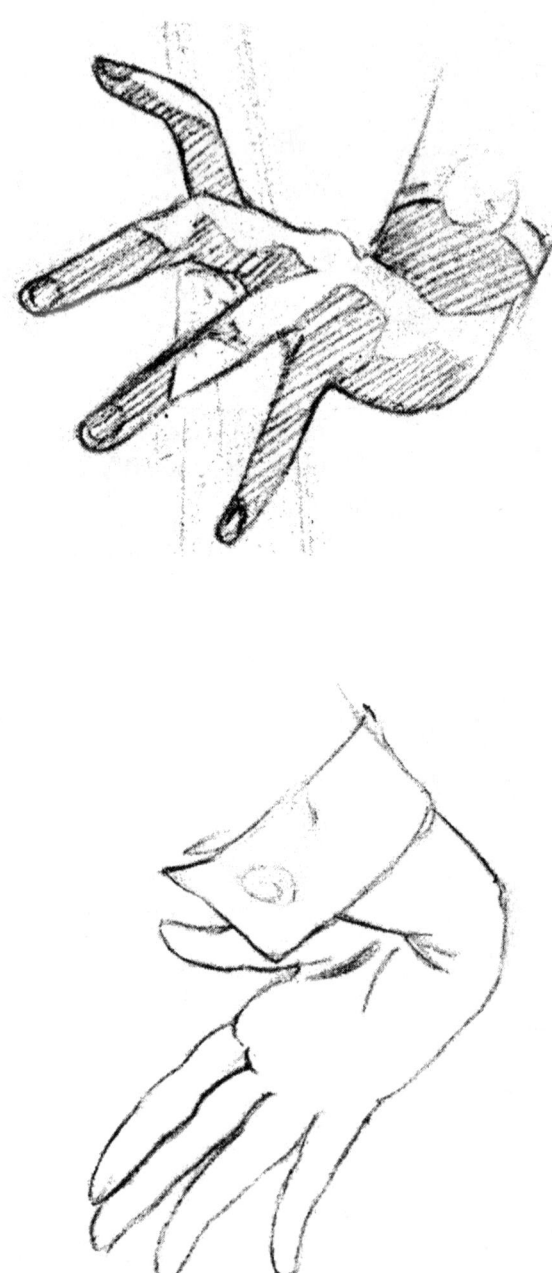

CHAPTER TWENTY-NINE
THE HAND

In the hand and foot, the bones of the fingers and toes are attached to a common center in somewhat the same manner as the ribs of a fan are held at the joint. As these bones are loose at one end, the number of positions that the finger may assume is very great. It is very confusing to try to draw the hands and feet unless they are considered as part of some orderly scheme.

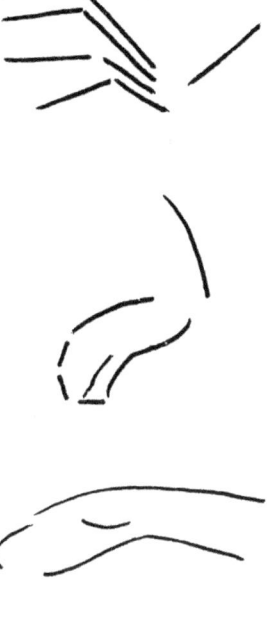

In the hand at top of the drawing on the left, the fingers have been considered as a decorative motive in which the lines radiate from the lines on the outside of the arm. The first finger swings into the curve at the heel of the hand, and extends up the lower side of the arm, while the lines from the other fingers seem to be extensions of the line of the top of the wrist.

In the other two hands it is obvious that the extension of line is toward the mechanical center and, all things being equal, it is safe to say that in any position where the fingers are spread and the hand is not violently foreshortened the line will point toward this common center.

The position of the ends of the fingers may be fixed by drawing a curve that will pass through the top of each and include them all. Here again it is often helpful to compare them to the sticks of a fan.

At first glance the hand seems the most difficult part of the human anatomy to draw, but it is so alluring as a decorative motive, and is so fascinating to draw, that it offers more than the usual inducements to the artist who works from it.

DIRECTIONS

Draw your own left hand in a mirror.

Draw the hands of the members of the class.

Search for the character in the hands of people about you. (It is expressed in two ways—by the position in which it rests and by its slope.)

Draw the hand of a lady and of a laborer, and compare them. As strength and beauty are often one, it may readily happen that the laborer's hand will be the more beautiful.

QUESTIONS: Why is the hand interesting to draw? Explain how the hand may be thought of as a decorative motive. How are the fingers drawn the right length? Of all the hands that you have seen, describe the most beautiful. How is it possible for a workman's hand to be beautiful? If the face expressed one character and the hand another, which would you think more likely to be real? Why? How is character expressed by the hand?

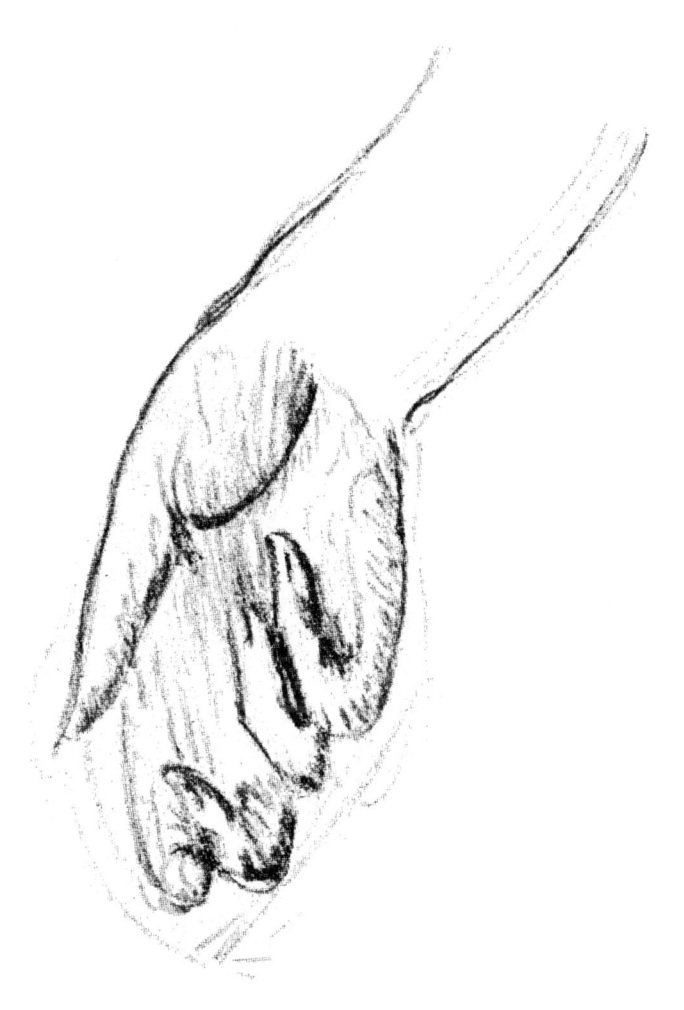

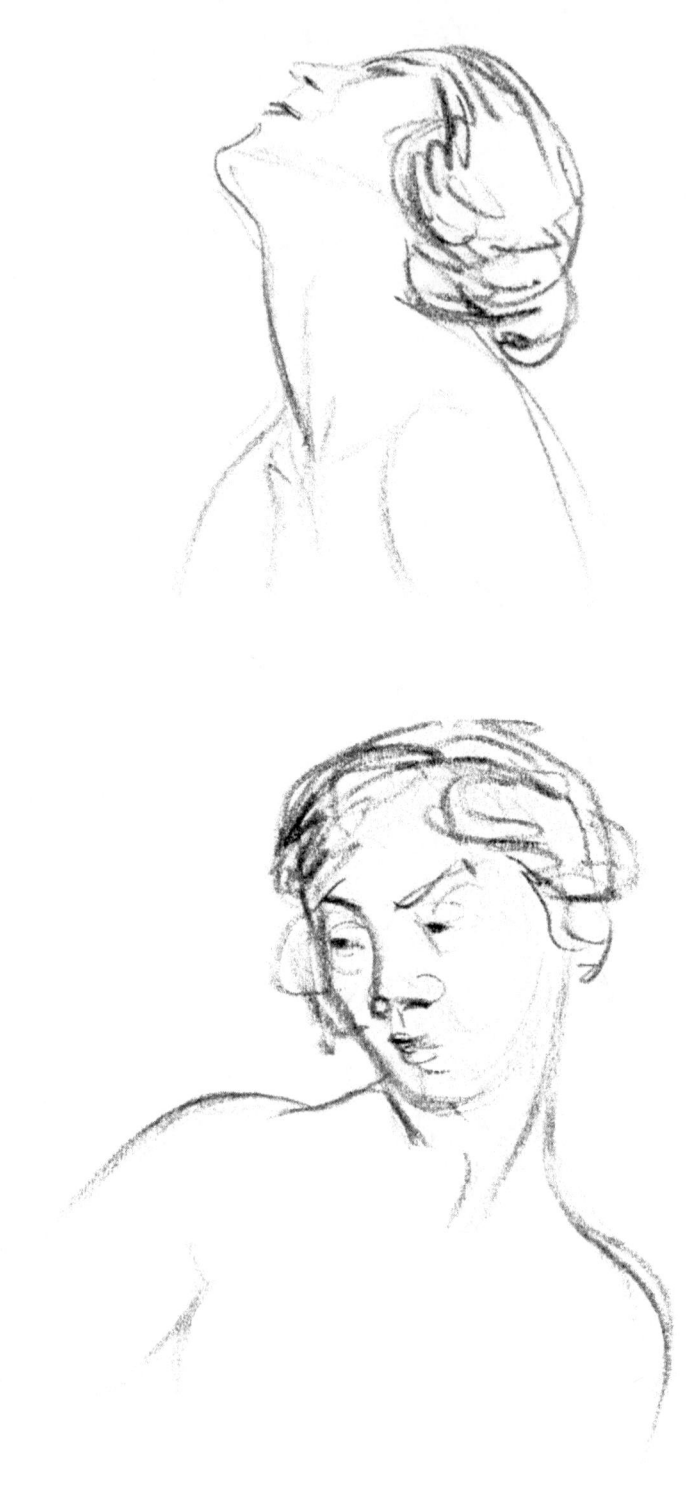

CHAPTER THIRTY
THE HEAD

When drawing the head, the real difficulty is in building it up into three dimensions, to make it seem to have depth and solidity. The difficulty lies not so much in shading the features as in bringing out the bony structure of the face and head.

In the matter of solidity, very few modern draftsmen can compete with the old masters. In the modern world of art it is safe to say that while there are many who can draw the features skillfully, there are only a few who can draw the head with real power.

It is, therefore, advisable that the student should resist as long as possible the temptation to draw "languorous" eyes and cupid-bow mouths, and that he should spend the early stages of his study in ascertaining the structural possibilities of the head in relation to light. A close study of the drawings of da Vinci, Raphael, and Michelangelo, will give the student an idea of how light and shade are best handled.

In drawing the head and shading it, do not adhere too strictly to the four-minute periods (although the heads given on the opposite page were made in that time), but complete them in the shortest time compatible with careful study.

DIRECTIONS

Draw the same head from memory in the same period of time.

Try to pose the head of a fellow student in the same position and light, and draw in the same time.

Draw the same head from memory in the same period of time.

Try to draw the head of the model or of a fellow student in the same time.

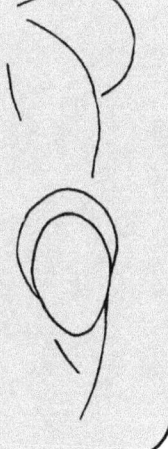

QUESTIONS: Why was the student asked to study Chapter Seven? Why is it thought better at first to study the shape of the head rather than the features? What could the old masters do that seems to surpass us? Why do you think this is so? Why is it a temptation to draw the features at once? Does the beginner know less of the shape of the head or the shape of the features? Why is it better to make drawings look like people rather than like pictures? What has this course taught you beyond the practice in drawing the figure?

ADDENDUM
PHOTOGRAPHIC REFERENCES

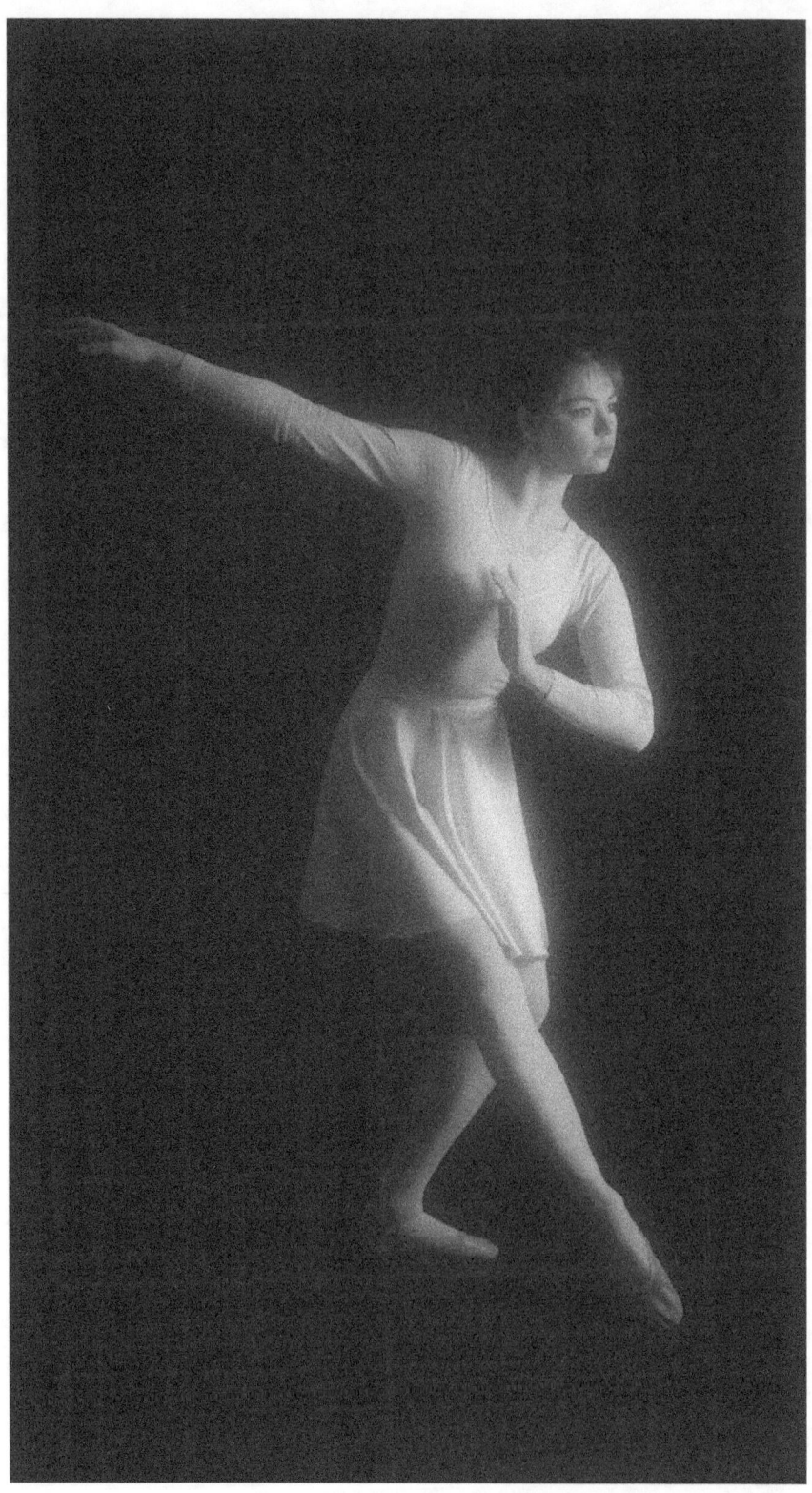

REFERENCE ONE
THE DANCER

This very beautiful photograph owes part of its very real beauty to the use of the soft focus lens which has eliminated detail until only the important lines attract the eye. This figure should be drawn from memory many times until its dominant lines are well fixed in the mind.

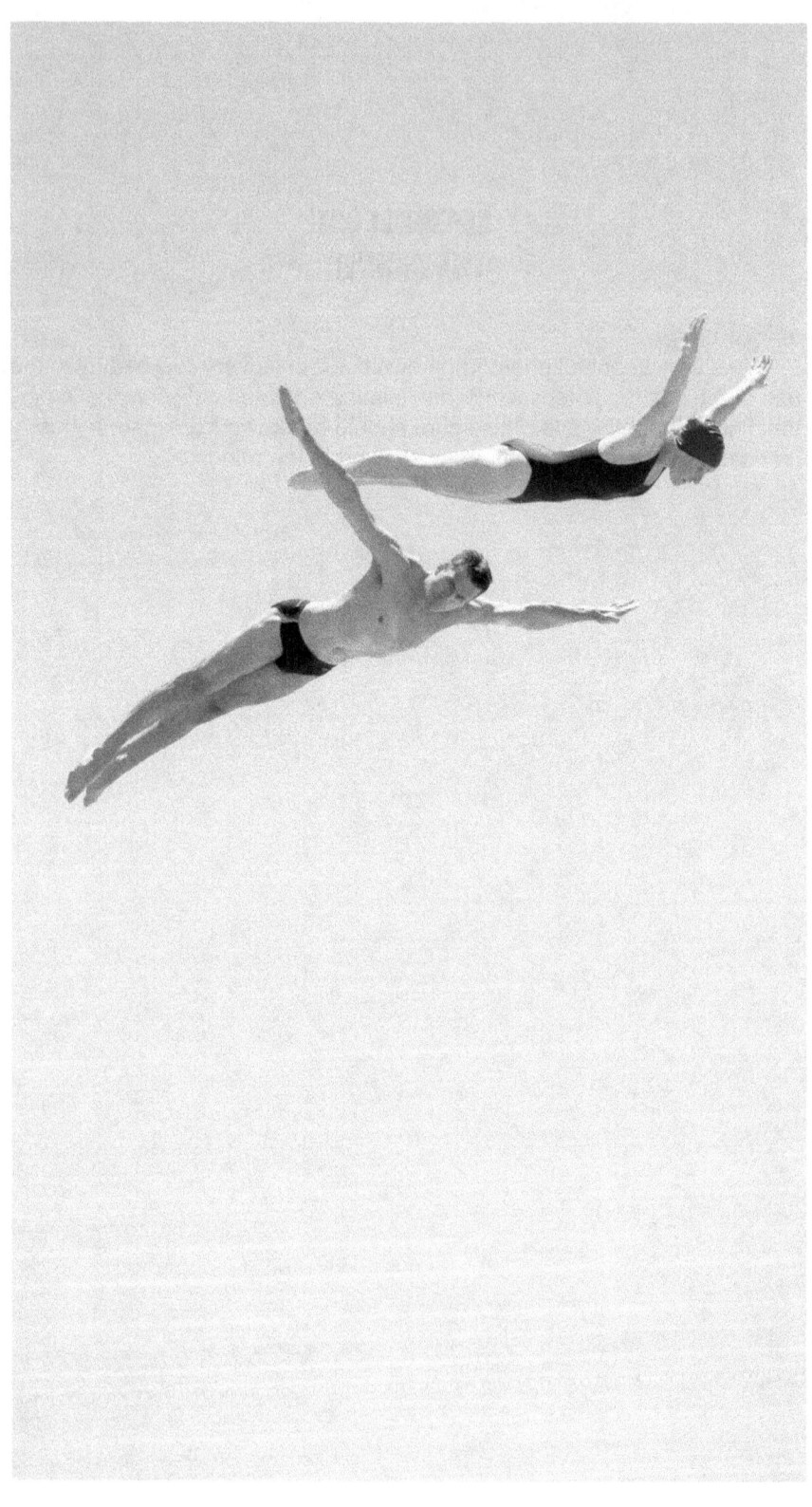

REFERENCE TWO
THE SWAN DIVE

The fine lines of the figure in the so-called Swan Dive are familiar to all those who are interested in aquatic sports. In this dive the body is pushed off from the springboard by the toes and legs without much spring and the body is held rigid during its descent, the arms being brought forward to protect the face only at the last moment. The turn during descent must be made with the greatest nicety of precision for, if the body is turned too far, it would mean a bad wrench to the back, followed by a dangerously deep plunge; and too slight a turn, a bad splash and a sore abdomen. In the image on the left, the two figures have just "taken off" and are beginning the descent in an almost horizontal position. The upper figure is particularly beautiful in its symmetry and line and in the bird-like attitude of arms and head. The student should study the balance of both figures for, in spite of there being no support on the ground, the center of gravity is perfectly fixed in order that the turn forward may be perfectly executed.

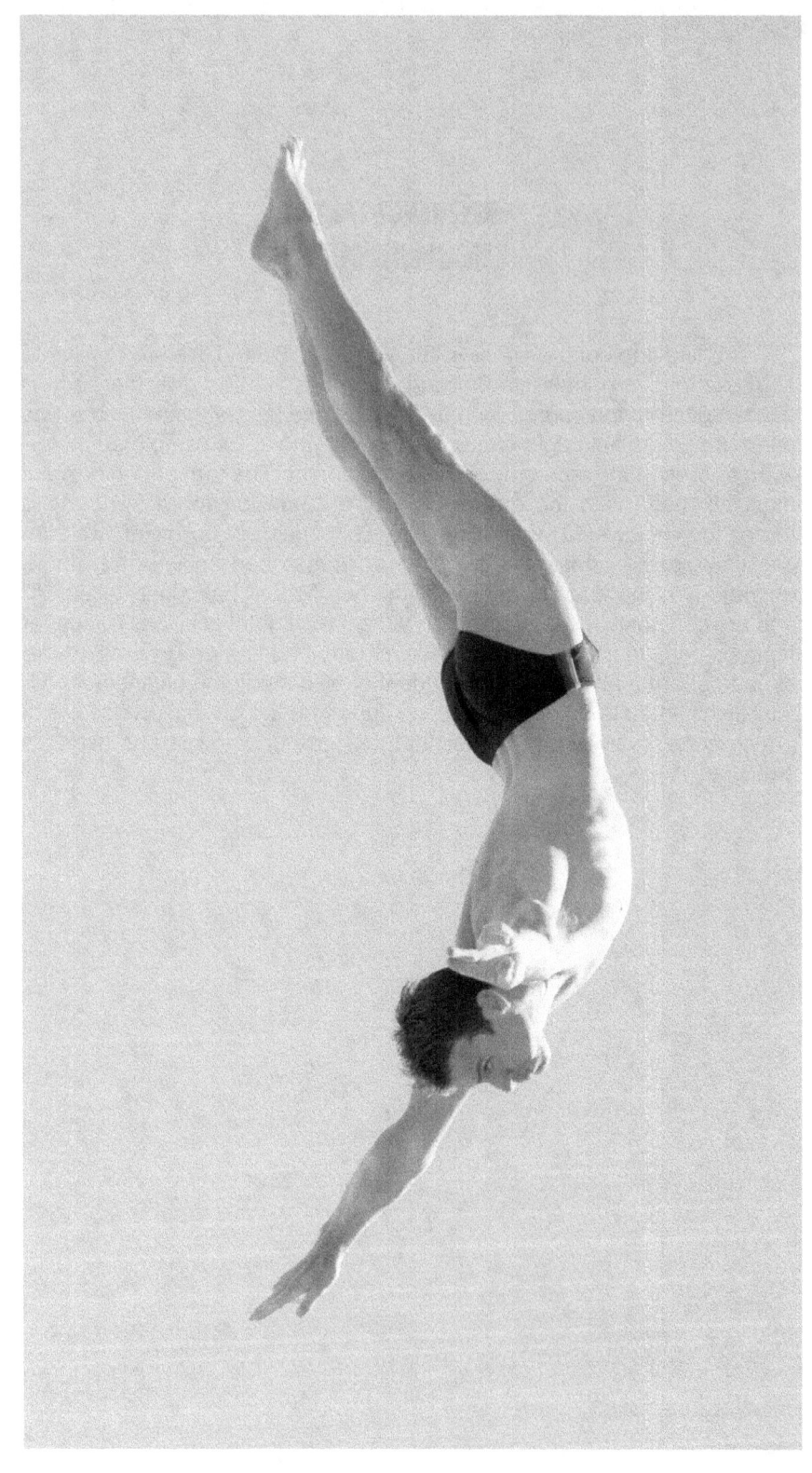

REFERENCE THREE
THE BACK DIVE

In the image on the left the figure is represented with the arms thrown forward just at the end of a back dive, the take off having been made with the body facing the spring board and thus turned backward in its descent. Even the toes are pointed to carry out the long lines of the figure and to make no splash in entering the water. The student should attempt to draw from imagination the various positions of a diver in both front and back dives from the top of the descent to the very last instant before the actual plunge, and should try to visualize the several positions of the arms.

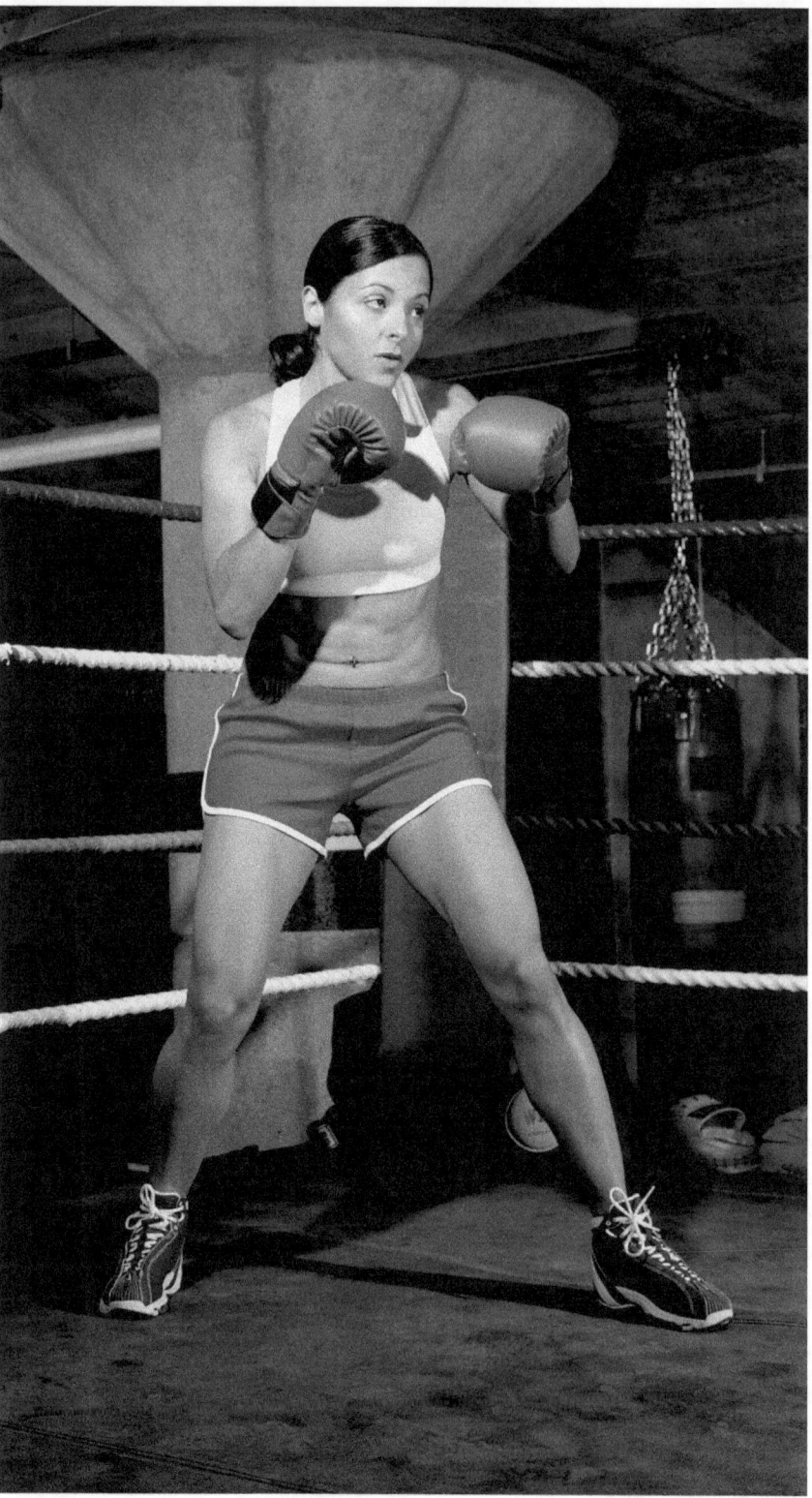

REFERENCE FOUR
THE BOXER

The accompanying photograph shows to advantage lines that express speed and power. It is the perfect position of the body that seems to give the impending blow its feeling of weight and it is this satisfactory correlation of the whole that gives the sense of grace.

In athletics today much attention is being given to what is called "perfect timing." "Perfect timing" insures that each part of the body shall be in its proper place at exactly the right time. In this case, the blow is obviously perfectly timed, for the body has arrived in the right position to give it its greatest power. While athletic instructors make a fine distinction between "perfect timing" and "perfect form," they are much the same to an outsider and they are blood brothers of grace and beauty.

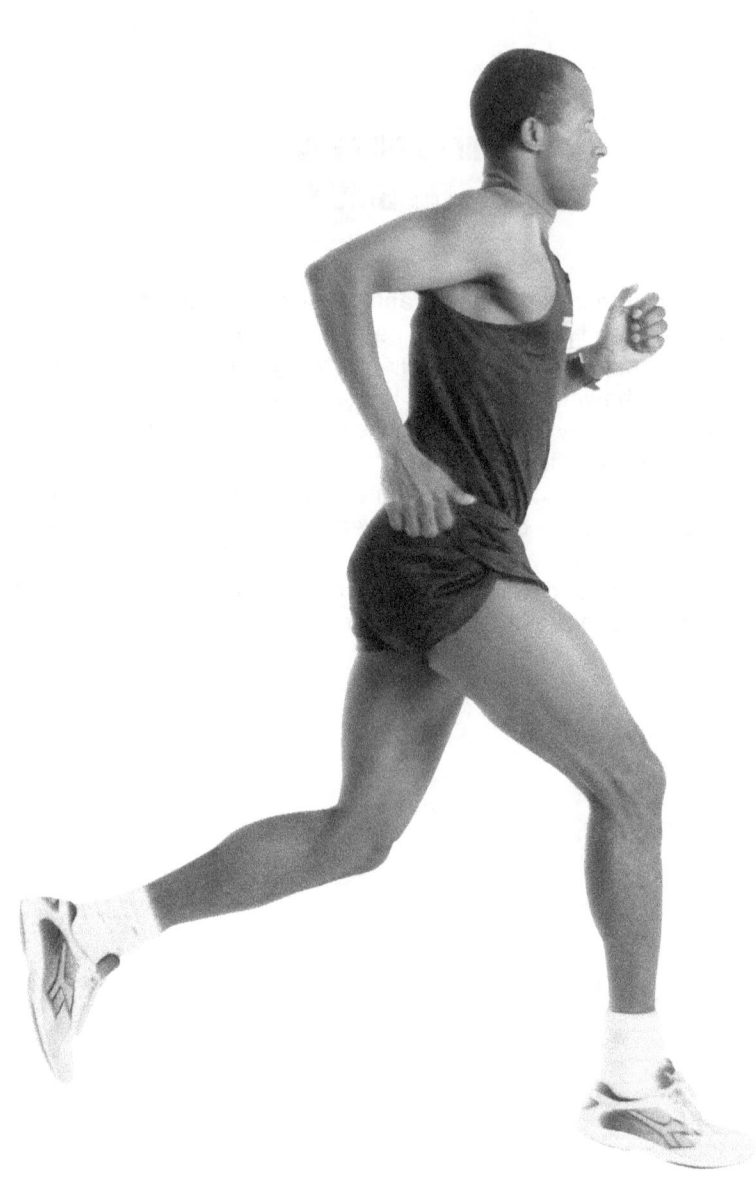

REFERENCE FIVE
THE RUNNER

If the runner is going in good "form," any attempt to change the position of a hand or an arm will seem to reduce his speed. It will be instructive for the student to attempt first to draw a person running fast, if possible, and then to reduce the speed by deliberately putting one part extremely out of place. Extreme effort is rarely genuinely beautiful and in this case, although the runner is in obvious good form, his contour being angular lacks the grace of the figures in less strenuous action. It will be observed that both feet are off the ground and that the right foot is just coming down to it. It is very important that details of this kind be understood and faithfully reproduced in studying motion.

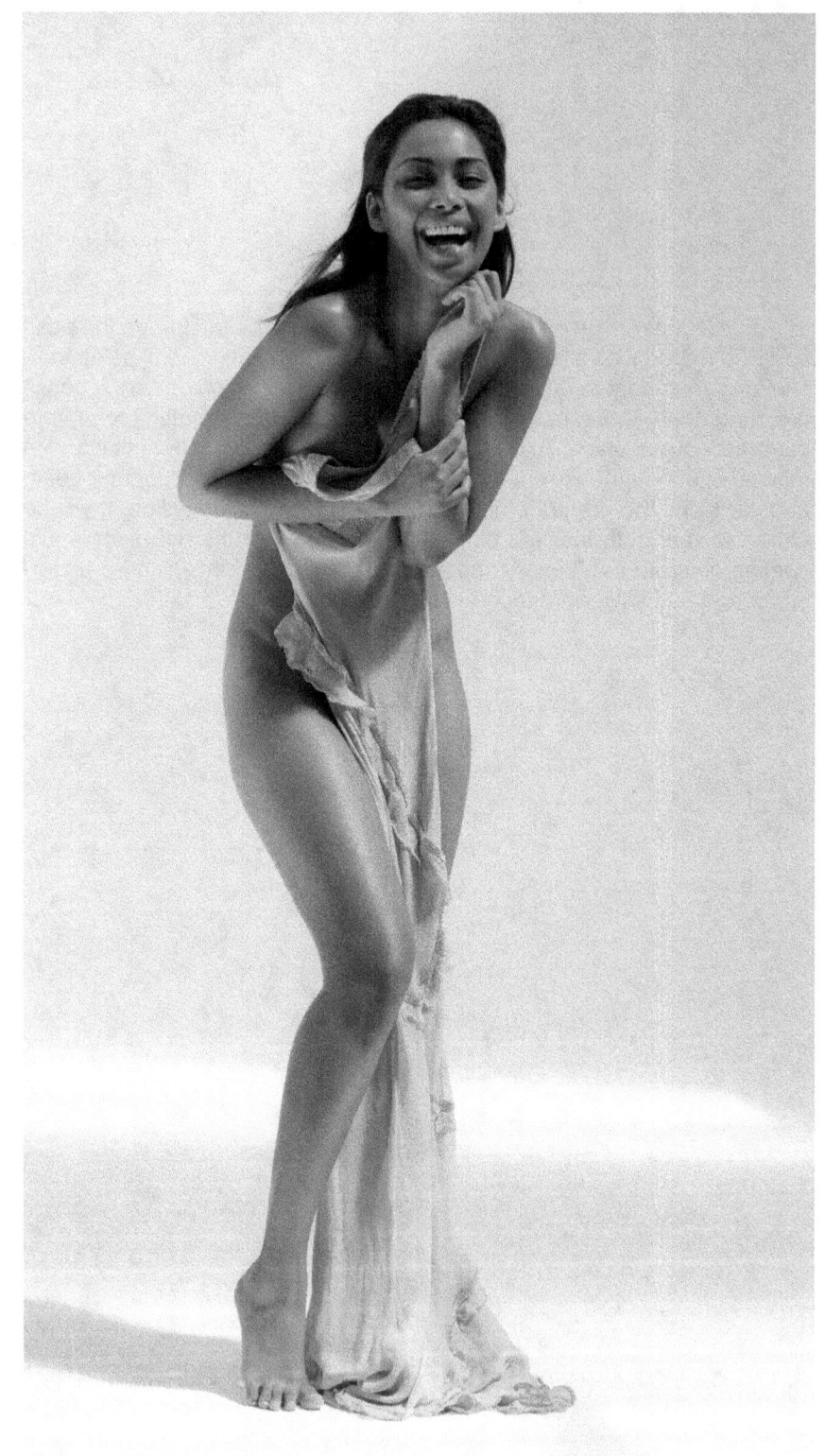

REFERENCE SIX
DRAPERY

Never has drapery as such been made as subservient to the figure as by the classic greek artists. In the image on the left, remniscent of classical greek structure, the satin practically duplicates every contour, and every line of it is drawn in sympathetic relation to the lines of the figure. This figure also serves as a particularly clear example of the theory advanced in Chapter Ten.

www.ingramcontent.com/pod-product-compliance
Lightning Source LLC
Chambersburg PA
CBHW072223170526
45158CB00002BA/721